COWBOYS

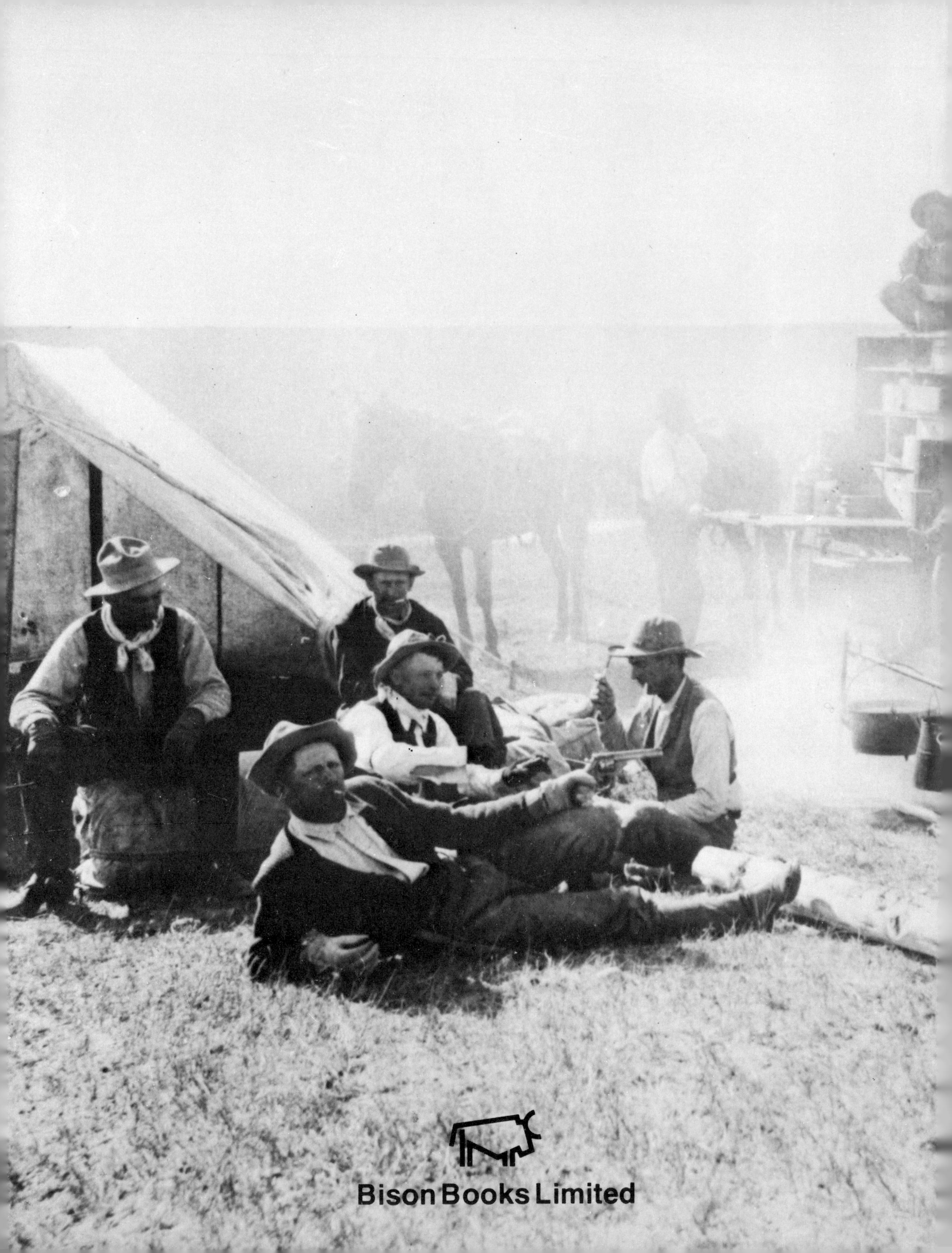

Bison Books Limited

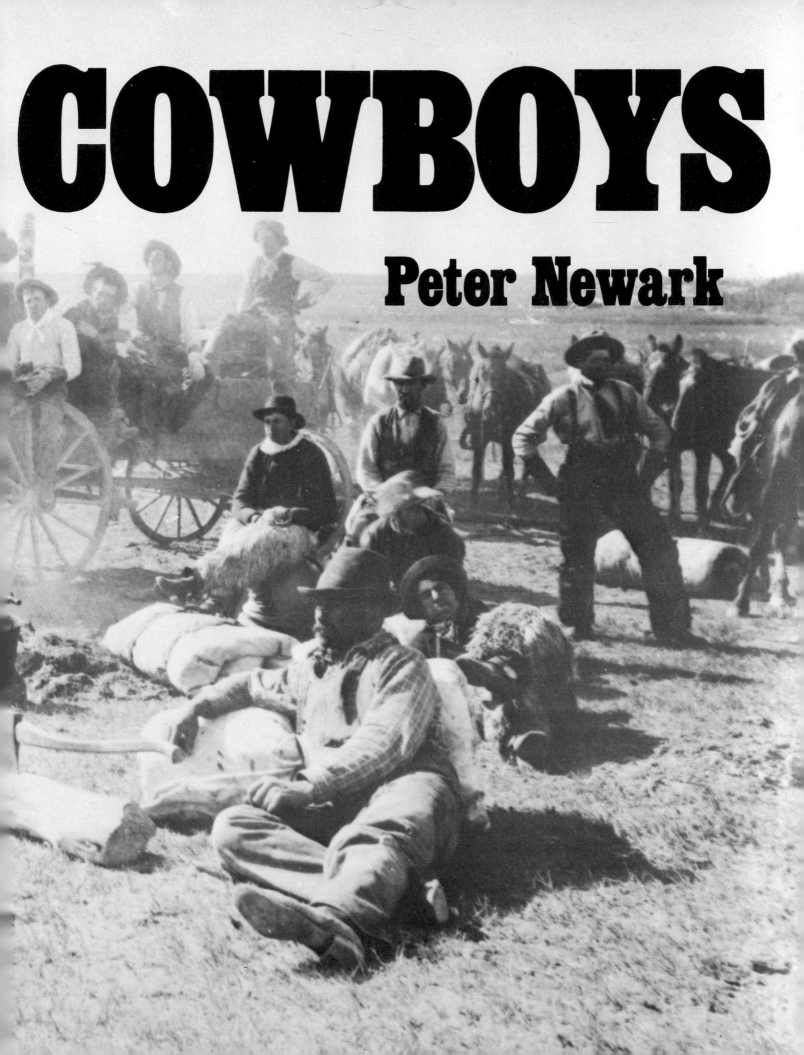

COWBOYS

Peter Newark

Published 1982 by
Bison Books Limited
39 Sloane Street, London SW1

Copyright © 1982 Bison Books Limited

ISBN 0 86124 044 8

Printed in Hong Kong

Page 1: *Morning Sun* by F T Johnson
Page 3: Wyoming cowboys relaxing at the
chuckwagon.
This page. If there had been such things as typical
cowboys, these men might have qualified. *(Men of
the Open Range*, C M Russell)

This book is dedicated to all the unknown working
cowboys who lived and died without fame or favor.

CONTENTS

William Frederick Cody—'Buffalo Bill'.

FOREWORD

The cowboy is the most romanticized, most misrepresented figure ever to ride across the pages of North American history. In the years immediately following the Civil War, the trail-driving cowboy—the original Texas type—quickly gained a reputation for wild behavior and violence, a transient troublemaker, rough and all too ready to use his sixshooter. As the years passed, this desperado was transformed by pulp writers, journalists, and Buffalo Bill's Wild West show into a colorful folk hero. Finally, the alchemists of Hollywood transmuted the base metal of a mounted workingman into an international star of the silver screen, a clean-cut cliché caballero, perhaps best represented by the fanciful figure of Tom Mix.

I do not subscribe to the belief that when truth and legend conflict, print the legend. In writing this factual account of the 19th century cowboy I have drawn largely on newspaper reports and journals of the time, on contemporary views of travelers and observers of the cattle country, and the published recollections of the cowboys themselves. I hereby acknowledge my literary debt to other authors I have consulted and give special thanks to the institutions, museums, friends and strangers who have contributed information and illustrations to this volume. Many of the pictures are from my own extensive collection of Western Americana.

Peter Newark

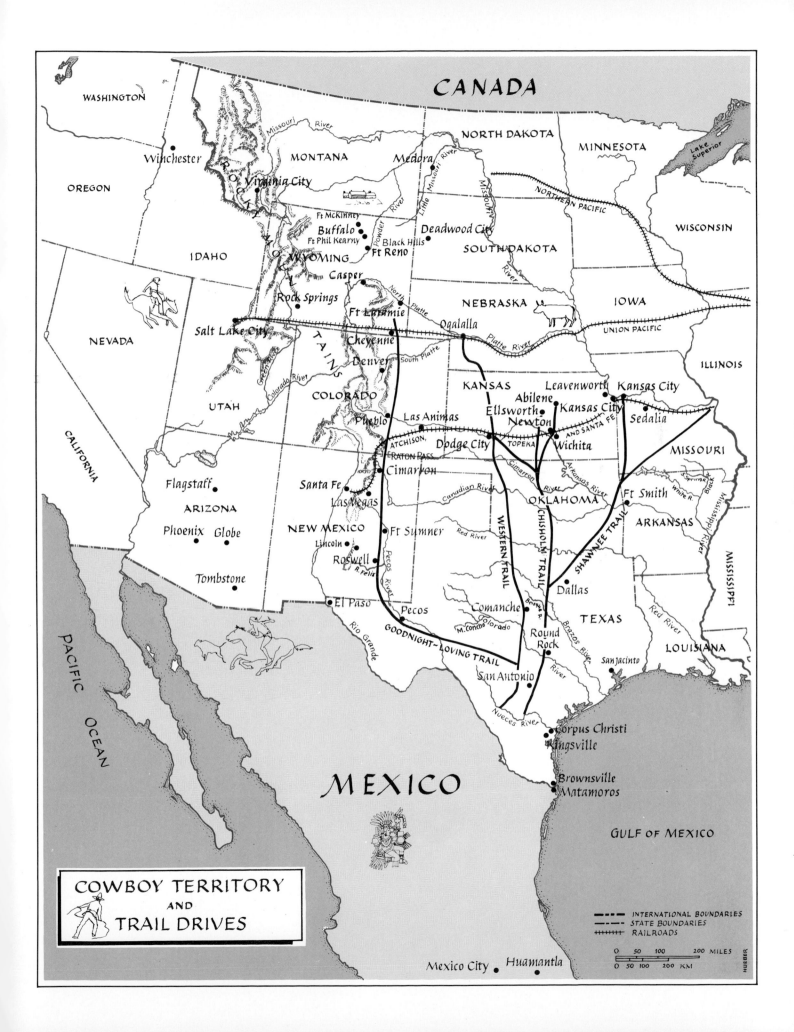

CANADA

WASHINGTON

OREGON

Winchester

MONTANA

Virginia City

Missouri River

Medora

NORTH DAKOTA

MINNESOTA

Lake Superior

IDAHO

Ft McKinney

Buffalo

Ft Phil Kearny

Black Hills

Ft Reno

Deadwood City

SOUTH DAKOTA

WISCONSIN

NORTHERN PACIFIC

WYOMING

Casper

Rock Springs

Ft Laramie

North Platte

NEBRASKA

IOWA

NEVADA

Salt Lake City

Cheyenne

Ogalalla

Platte River

UNION PACIFIC

Denver

South Platte

ILLINOIS

Colorado River

Green River

UTAH

COLORADO

KANSAS

Leavenworth

Kansas City

CALIFORNIA

Pueblo

Las Animas

Abilene

Ellsworth

Newton

Kansas City

Sedalia

Flagstaff

Santa Fe

ATCHISON,

RATON PASS

Cimarron

Dodge City

TOPEKA

Wichita

AND SANTA FE

MISSOURI

ARIZONA

Las Vegas

Cimarron River

Arkansas River

Ft Smith

S. Spring R.

White R.

Black R.

Mississippi River

Phoenix

Globe

NEW MEXICO

Ft Sumner

Canadian River

OKLAHOMA

ARKANSAS

MISSISSIPPI

Lincoln

Red River

WESTERN TRAIL

CHISHOLM TRAIL

SHAWNEE TRAIL

Roswell

R. Felix

Pecos River

Tombstone

El Paso

Pecos

Comanche

M. Concho

Colorado

Bosque R.

Dallas

Brazos River

TEXAS

Red River

LOUISIANA

PACIFIC OCEAN

Rio Grande

GOODNIGHT-LOVING TRAIL

Round Rock

River

San Jacinto

San Antonio

Nueces River

Corpus Christi

Kingsville

MEXICO

Brownsville

Matamoros

GULF OF MEXICO

COWBOY TERRITORY
AND
TRAIL DRIVES

Mexico City

Huamantla

- - - INTERNATIONAL BOUNDARIES
- · - STATE BOUNDARIES
++++ RAILROADS

0   50   100   200 MILES
0 50 100   200 KM

HUEBER

United States Army Dragoons in Texas charging an enemy gun battery in the Battle of Resaca de la Palma, which occurred 9 May 1846 and was a turning point in the Mexican War.

1
THE FIRST COWBOYS

Young Texas now is free,
And when I shine among the stars,
How happy I shall be.

Song of Texas, circa 1848

The story of the Anglo-American cowboy begins in Texas, the cradle of the great cattle-raising industry that, in 30 years, fanned out from the Lone Star State to the far northern plains and other Western territories. In the sunburned wilderness of Texas, frontier man, mustang horse and Longhorn cattle, rawhide and leather, spurs, sombrero and six-shooter coalesced to form the distinctive figure of the Texas cowboy, the paradigm of all other American cowboys that followed him. The Texas cowboy's independent character and Viking spirit were forged in the flames of revolt against Mexican rule and tempered by the Indian-fighting, trouble-shooting tradition of the hard-riding Texas Rangers.

'Cow-boys can be divided into two classes,' commented an observer in 1880. 'Those hailing from the Lone Star State . . . the others recruited either from Eastern States, chiefly Missouri, or from the Pacific slopes . . . The Texans are, as far as true cow-boyship goes, unrivalled; [they are] the best riders, hardy, and born to the business. The others are less able but more orderly men. The bad name of [the] Texans arises mostly from their excitable tempers, and the fact that they are mostly "on the shoot"—that is, very free in the use of their revolvers.'

The original Texas cowboy was a synthesis of Spanish, Mexican and Anglo-American cultures. His particular form owes much to the Spanish occupation of North America and their development of the New World. The Conquistadors and early Spanish colonists introduced domesticated cattle and horses into North America; both types of animal being unknown to the native Indian population. In mastering the mustang, the Plains Indians transformed themselves from a hitherto pedestrian people into skilled equestrian hunters of the bison or buffalo that roamed the prairies in the millions.

The word 'mustang' derives from the Spanish *mesteños*, meaning horses that had escaped from a mesta or group of stock-raisers. These horses ran wild and multiplied, the Western plains being natural horse (and cattle) country. They evolved into a hardy, wiry, ill-formed breed of small horses, rarely 14 hands (4' 8'') high. In similar fashion numbers of Spanish cattle ran off into (or were abandoned in) the wild. They propagated, and evolved into the Texas Longhorn, a distinctive breed of which we shall read more in the following chapter. The Longhorn is the linchpin of the cowboy story; handling these cattle was the way of life of the Texas cowboy.

By the 18th century the aggressive and adventurous Spaniards, greedy for gold and imperial territory, had conquered the whole of Mexico, California and Texas; the latter gaining its name because the Indians were friendly to the Spaniards, who called them *tejas*, meaning 'friends' or 'allies,' thus the country became known as 'the land of the Tejas,' and later, Texas. Spanish settlers began cattle ranching here, mostly in the triangle of land between the Nueces River, the Rio Grande and the Gulf of Mexico. These *ranchos* were run in the same free range manner as those in Mexico. The cattle were allowed to wander far and wide over the unfenced open range to graze and breed. And because cattle from different owners intermingled on the plains, a system of branding was introduced to identify the animals by the owner's individual mark. With the grazing animals ranging over such a vast area, horsemen had to be employed to tend and round up the cattle when necessary.

The Spanish ranchers recruited half-civilized mission Indians and halfbreeds to look after the herds. These hardy and humble cow herders were called *vaqueros* (from the Spanish *vaca* for cow) and over the years they developed traditional skills and know-how in managing cattle from horseback. They roped the animals with *la reata* (whence the American 'lariat'), a rawhide rope with a running noose, and they developed gear and equipment suitable to their particular equestrian life. Too poor to afford boots, these early *vaqueros* strapped huge Spanish spurs to their bare or sandaled feet; and, brought up in the saddle, they seldom walked if they could ride. They wore wide-brimmed hats to ward off the sun and leather aprons to protect their legs from the thorny chaparral brush. Proud of his calling

Opposite top: Mexican *vaqueros*, or cowboys, roping and branding cattle. Center: The Spaniards brought cattle into Texas (illustration by José Cisneros). Bottom right: A Mexican *vaquero* from a drawing of 1850. Bottom left: *A Mexican Vaquero*— an illustration by Frederic Remington.

and fiercely loyal to his herd and master, the *vaquero* spread his influence throughout the southwest and California.

While the Spanish established their empire on the west coast and in the southwest of North America, the English, Dutch and French colonized the east coast. The English ousted the Dutch and dominated the French. In time the English-speaking colonists rebelled against British rule and created the United States of America. The French still held the vast undeveloped territory of Louisiana, lying between the Mississippi River and the Rocky Mountains, from Canada to the Gulf of Mexico. When in 1803 the United States purchased this great tract of land from France, the size of the infant republic was almost doubled. By the middle of the century streams of wagon trains were rolling westward from the Mississippi carrying settlers to the far wilderness. The Winning of the West had begun.

In 1820 Moses Austin was granted permission by the Spanish authorities to establish a colony of 300 Anglo-American families in the virtually uninhabited land of Texas. Moses Austin died

The cowboy had problems other than herding cattle, such as hostile Indians.

before he could carry out his plans and his son Stephen completed the task, settling the families on the rich farm and pasture land along the banks of the Colorado River. When Mexico freed herself of the Spanish yoke in 1821 Texas came under Mexican rule. In those early years Stephen Austin was the undisputed leader of the growing colony, being lawmaker, chief judge and military commander; he dealt with the Indians, charted the province, encouraged industry and promoted commerce with the U.S. and stimulated a steady flow of Anglo-American immigrants into Texas.

The settlers were in constant conflict with the Indians—Lipan, Kiowa, and Comanche—especially the latter. Austin hired a band of horsemen to range over the country to scout the movements of hostile Indians and this duty gave rise to the Texas Ranger force, of which more later. Alarmed at the growing numbers of Anglos settling in Texas, the Mexican government tried to stop the tide in 1830. This action and other repressive measures (as Anglos viewed it) gave rise to the Texas War of Independence. The new Texans brought with them the industry and thrift that characterized the frontier American, and his spirit of independence and capacity for self-government. The Texans also possessed the Anglo prejudice against the Indian and dislike and contempt for the Spaniard.

From the outset the Texans assumed a racial superiority over the Mexican 'greaser,' a derogatory term that originated in the days when Anglo-American traders bought hides and tallow from the Spaniards in California. In return, the Mexicans referred to the Anglos as 'gringos,' an uncomplimentary name derived from the Spanish *griego* for Greek, meaning a foreigner who spoke 'Greek' or an unintelligible language. Compelling the rebellious Texans to respect Mexican law and government was made extremely difficult because of the colony's isolation from the national capital of Mexico City.

Stephen Austin was imprisoned by the Mexicans for a year and released in 1835. Later that year the Texans rose in revolt and Austin was called upon to command the small volunteer army. He led a successful campaign against San Antonio. In December 1835 he was sent to the US on a diplomatic mission to enlist aid and volunteers. On 23 February 1836 a Mexican army, 5000-strong, commanded by General Antonio Lopez de Santa Ana, President of Mexico, entered San Antonio and laid siege to the fortified mission of the Alamo, held by a garrison of some 180 men, which included the noted frontiersmen James Bowie (of Bowie knife fame) and Davy Crockett. The gallant defenders gave fierce resistance and managed to hold out for 13 days until crushed by the final assault at dawn on 6 March; all the defenders fought to the death. The Mexicans, however, had won a Pyrrhic victory, suffering more than 1500 casualties, causing one of Santa Ana's generals to remark: 'Another such victory and we are ruined.'

Below: A painting by H Charles McBarron, *The Battle of the Alamo*. Inset: A night view of the floodlit Alamo as it is today, standing in downtown San Antonia, Texas.

Texan vengeance came 46 days after the fall of the Alamo, when General Sam Houston, with an army of less than 800 volunteers, defeated Santa Ana and his army of 1300 at San Jacinto. Before joining battle, Houston exhorted his men: 'Some of us may be killed, must be killed; but, soldiers, remember the Alamo! The Alamo! The Alamo!' The Texans fought with such ferocity that they completely routed the Mexicans in a matter of minutes, killing 600 while losing only eight. This stunning triumph freed Texas from Mexican rule and a Republic was declared in October 1836, with Sam Houston its first president.

The early Anglo settlers in Texas were primarily farmers, and cattle ranching was at first not important to them. With the establishment of the Republic of Texas, the Mexican ranchers, under harrassment from encroaching Texans, abandoned their *ranchos* and many of their cattle and retired to safety over the Rio Grande. The Texans moved into the cattle country and took over the property and stock the Mexicans had left behind. When the new republic declared all unbranded cattle public property, Texans, assisted by remaining *vaqueros*, began to round up the wild Longhorns and brand them with their own marks. These

Above (left to right): Stephen Austin (1793-1836), the founder of Texas; Captain Samuel Walker, who helped design the Walker-Colt revolver; W J 'Bill' McDonald, a famous captain of the Texas Rangers. Right: Texas Rangers of the 1890s. Left to right: Bob Speaker, Jim Putnam, Lon Odam and Sergeant John R Hughes.

Anglo range riders adopted and adapted the methods, dress and equipment of the *vaquero*, and many of the Spanish-Mexican words he used, and in the following years developed the skills, character and life style that comprised the Texas cowboy.

But why the name 'cowboy' in particular? Why not 'cowman' or 'cow herder,' or 'stock boy' or 'cow driver' or 'trail rider'? Well, indeed they were called all these things in their time but 'cowboy' is the one that stuck and came into general use about a century ago. It is an appropriate appellation, as most cowboys were young. The term started to appear in the popular press about 1870 and for a number of years it was always hyphenated and enclosed in quotation marks. A journalist of 1873 informed his readers that 'The "Cow-Boys" of Texas are a peculiar breed. They are distinct in their habits

Opposite top: Sometimes an individual animal would break away from the herd and have to be rounded up *(The Bolter* by C M Russell). Bottom: Cowboys fighting off an Indian attack (from an illustration by Frederic Remington).

and characteristics from the remainder of even the Texas population as if they belonged to another race. The Lipan and Comanche are not unlike the civilized white man than is the nomadic herdsman to the Texan who dwells in the city or cultivates the plains.'

The origin of the term 'cowboy' can be traced back to Revolutionary days, when guerrillas plundered the New York area stealing supplies and livestock for the British. In the *Pictorial Field Book of the Revolution* published in 1850, Benson Lossing tells us that 'The party called Cow-Boys were mostly refugees belonging to the British side, and engaged in plundering the people near the lines of their cattle and driving them to New York.' The first use of the term in Texas is open to argument. Some say it was applied to a wild bunch of riders led by Ewen Cameron who harassed the Mexican ranchers and fought the Indians during the early days of the Texas Republic and became known as 'Cameron's Cowboys.'

It seems that early Texas usage of the name 'cowboy' was synonymous with 'bandit' or 'robber.' Charles W Webber in *Tales of the Southern Border*, 1868, writes: 'The old man was a cattle driver, or "cow-boy," as those men are and were termed who drove in the cattle of the Mexican *rancheros* of the Rio Grande border, either by stealth, or after plundering or murdering the herdsman. They were, in short, considered as banditti before the Revolution, and have been properly considered so since.' After the Civil War, 'cowboy' came to signify anyone who tended cattle out West, but the name still retained a connotation of wildness; it was much, much later that 'cowboy' spelled romantic adventure.

The popular term 'cowpuncher' came into use in the mid-1880s when cowboys employed prodpoles to urge cattle through chutes into railroad cars, and often had to 'punch' those animals onto their feet that had got down in the crowded car; 'cowpoke' is another version of cowpuncher. A cowboy was also called a 'buckeroo,' a corruption of *vaquero.* 'Cattle-man' and 'rancher' were always used to denote an owner or raiser of cattle; at the top of the league were the 'cattle kings' or 'barons.'

'The original cow-boy of this country,' wrote Joseph Nimmo, Jr, in *The American Cow-Boy,* in the November, 1886 issue of *Harper's New Monthly Magazine*, 'was essentially a creature of circumstance, and mainly a product of western and south-western Texas. Armed to the teeth, booted and spurred, long-haired, and covered with the broad-brimmed sombrero—the distinctive badge of his calling—his personal appearance proclaimed the sort of man he was. The Texas cow-boys were frontiersmen, accustomed from their earliest child-hood to the alarms and the struggles incident to forays of Indians of the most ferocious and warlike nature. The section of the State in which they lived was also for many years exposed to incursions of bandits from Mexico, who came with predatory intent upon the herds and the homes of the people of Texas . . . But the peculiar characteristics of the Texas cow-boys qualified them for an important public service. By virtue of their courage and recklessness of danger, their excellent horsemanship, and skill in the use of firearms . . . they have been efficient in preventing Indian outbreaks and in protecting the frontier settlements.'

The Texas Rangers are part and parcel of the Texas cowboy story. The Rangers were the first to adopt Samuel Colt's early revolver; many cowboys volunteered for Ranger service and many Rangers, after their period of service, took up ranching. John R Hughes was a cowboy, a rancher, then a Ranger. Born in Illinois, he went to the Indian Territory (Oklahoma) and lived with the Indians for several years, learning to track animals and men. In 1878, working as a cowboy in Texas, he drove cattle up the trail to Kansas. He then started his own horse ranch in central Texas. In 1884 thieves ran off 70 of his horses and Hughes went after the gang alone. After a long trail he caught up with the six men in New Mexico and in the ensuing gunfight killed four of them and, in his own words, 'took the two surviving robbers to the nearest town and delivered them to the authorities.' He returned to his ranch with the stolen horses, having been away just under a year and traveling 1200 miles. It was this inci-

Left: An advertisement for Colt firearms painted in 1925 by Frank E Schoonover. Above: One of the dangers of the cattle drive was the possibility of a stampede (*Cattle Stampede* by Robert Lindneux).

Above: The buffalo was almost extinct by 1900 (*The Still Hunt* by J H Moser, 1888). Right: An eastern view of the rough and ready men of the West. This cartoon of 1861 shows a wild and hairy Texas Ranger loaded with weapons.

In this photograph made by A A Brack of San Antonio in the 1880s, a cowboy in his 40 dollar saddle on his 20 dollar horse.

An early engraving of an American cowboy in Texas looking after his cattle. Notice the immense rowel on the spur.

dent that led him to join the Rangers, in which he served for 28 years, from 1887 to 1915, and rose to the rank of captain. Such was his reputation in the force that journalists dubbed him the 'Bayard of the Chaparral' and 'Boss of the Border.'

W J 'Bill' McDonald, former cowboy and rancher, was a celebrated Ranger captain of the 1890s. He embodied the fighting spirit of the force. It is said that on one occasion when called on to deal with a mob situation he turned up alone. 'Where are the other Rangers?' asked the local authority.

'You ain't got but one riot, have you?' replied the taciturn McDonald.

His tenacious courage was best demonstrated when he engaged in a gunfight with three desperadoes led by a man named Mathews. Having been shot in the lung by Mathews, the Ranger fired back and fatally wounded the man. Then the other two gunmen started shooting at McDonald, hitting him twice in the left arm and in the right side. With the fingers of his gun hand numbed, the Ranger could not cock the hammer of his single-action Colt, so he raised the revolver to his mouth and pulled back the hammer with his teeth; this deter-

mined action so unnerved his opponents that they turned and fled. McDonald recovered from his wounds and in 1897 was instrumental in smashing the notorious Bill Ogle gang of San Saba County.

> He ne'er would sleep within a tent,
> No comforts would he know;
> But like a brave old Texican,
> A-ranging he would go.
> *Ballad of Mustang Gray*

The Texas Rangers originated in 1823 when Stephen Austin hired a band of horsemen to range over the country to scout the movements of hostile Indians, and this ranging duty gave the name to the force that became fully established during the period of the Texas Republic, 1836–45. Organized into companies with a captain commanding each company, the Rangers were self-reliant individuals who knew no military discipline; they never drilled or saluted their officers, and accepted a leader only if he proved the best in endurance, courage, and judgment. They wore no uniform and dressed in frontier style. Each man provided his own horse and equipment. What they lacked in military discipline they made up in remarkable riding and fighting ability. A Texas Ranger was defined as one who 'can ride like a Mexican, trail like an Indian, shoot like a Tennessean, and fight like a devil!'

For half a century the Rangers engaged in a continuous war with the fierce Comanches, probably the finest horsemen among the Plains Indians. In the early years the single-shot muzzle-loaded guns of the Rangers were inadequate against the bow and arrows of the Comanche, who could discharge a stream of arrows at his foe while at the gallop. The Rangers gained a great advantage over the Indians when they came into possession of Samuel Colt's revolver, an early five-shot model. Armed with two of these revolvers, one Ranger now had the firepower of 10 men armed with a single-shot weapon. The Colt was an ideal horseman's weapon and the Rangers used it with surprising and devastating effect against the Indians.

The first battle in which Colt revolvers were used against the Comanches took place at Pedernales in June 1844 when Captain Jack Coffee Hays and 14 Rangers clashed with about 70 redskins. The Comanches were accustomed to facing single-shot weapons, and when these had been discharged and were being reloaded,

the Indians would charge. But this time, instead of taking up a defensive position, Hays led his men in a spirited charge, taking heavy toll at close quarters with their repeating pistols. More than 30 Indians were killed and the others put to flight. Hays modestly gave the credit for the victory to the 'wonderful marksmanship of every Ranger, and the total surprise of the Indians, caused by the new six-shooters, which they had never seen or heard of before.'

The first six-shot Colt revolver was the .44 caliber 'Walker' Model of 1847, so called because Samuel Colt designed the weapon along lines suggested to him by Ranger Captain Samuel H Walker. The US government ordered 1000 of this new model for use in the Mexican War of 1846-48, a war triggered when Texas joined the Union in 1845 and the United States claimed the Rio Grande as its southern boundary with Mexico. The Mexicans disputed this and war resulted. Since the Rangers had long experience in fighting the Mexicans, General Zachary Taylor employed them as scouts and skirmishers. Captain Sam Walker, according to N C Brooks, in *A Complete History of the Mexican War*, 1849, used his Walker Colt with great effect:

In an illustration from the 1880s, two Texas Rangers arrest a Mexican outlaw in a cantina.

Below right: R H Williams, an Englishman who lived in Texas, ran a ranch and joined the Rangers.

Above: Texas cowboys roping a longhorn steer while their partners tend the rest of the herd.

Opposite: *The Bronco Buster* by Frederic Remington. Inset: *Cattle Drive from Texas.*

'Foremost of all in this noble charge was the gallant Walker. Firing his revolvers with a cool, steady, equable movement, his unerring hand brought down an enemy with every shot . . . he kept his place in the advance, and whenever the enemy attempted to make a stand, dashed upon him with a cry of triumph, and tore a bloody pathway through.' Walker was killed in action at Huamantla in October 1847: 'He died with a smoking Colt revolver in his hand.'

The United States won the war, which was formally ended by the Treaty of Guadalupe Hidalgo in February 1848. Mexico lost far more than a war. By the terms of the treaty she relinquished all claims to Texas above the Rio Grande, and ceded to the US the lands of New Mexico (including the present states of Arizona, New Mexico, Utah, Nevada, and parts of Wyoming and Colorado) and Upper California (the present State of California). In return for this vast acquisition, the victorious United States agreed to pay Mexico 15 million dollars. The Colt revolver attained national fame in the Mexican War. Indeed, the Rangers' enthusiasm for the weapon had saved Samuel Colt from going out of business for lack of orders.

'I am indebted to Texas,' Colt wrote in a letter to Sam Houston, 'for the development of the advantages my arms possess over the common arms of service. To Texans, I owe the orders I received for arming the first regiment of US Mounted Rifles of which the celebrated Colonel Walker holds a Captain's Commission. I am also indebted to Colonel Hays and other distinguished Texas officers now raising regiments and companies to fight in Mexico for late applications and requisitions on our Government for these arms . . . Texas has done more for me and my arms than all the country. Besides, they have a better knowledge of their use and want every Texas Ranger, in Mexico, to be thus armed before they are furnished any other troops.'

Thus did the Colt six-shooter and the Texas Ranger become inseparable. And the Colt and the cowboy became synonymous. When Texas seceded from the Union in 1861 and many Texans marched off to serve the Confederacy, the Rangers had to fight hard to protect the isolated, unmanned communities from the depredations of the Comanches. Charles Goodnight, cowboy and later cattle king, served in the

Top: Texas Rangers attacking a Comanche village (Illustration by Frederic Remington in *Harper's New Monthly* magazine, 1896). Above: Texas Ranger J B Armstrong, who captured the outlaw John Wesley Hardin in 1877.

proliferated to the enormous number of some five million head. Texas was poor but had this great reservoir of beef. The north was rich in industry but short of meat to feed its huge and hungry population. So began the period of the long trail drives north from Texas that is dealt with in the following chapter.

The end of the Civil War also brought a time of lawlessness to Texas. The Reconstruction forces took over the Texas government and the State had little control over its own destiny. The Ranger strength was reduced and a new state police force established, a force that proved to be corrupt, inefficient and widely despised. As a result the frontier became unsafe and Mexican bandits were encouraged to cross the Rio Grande and steal cattle. When Texas outlaw John Wesley Hardin was interviewed in jail in 1877 he told the reporter that his first trouble with the law had come with the state police: 'The Yankees and the state police got after me and tried to arrest me without a warrant.' The state police was abolished in April 1873, much to the delight of all Texans. 'The people of Texas,' announced the *Dallas Herald*, going on to mix metaphors in grand style, 'are today delivered from as infernal an engine of oppression as ever crushed any people beneath the heel of God's sunlight.'

In 1874, when the Texas legislature was returned to the hands of responsible men, a bill

Rangers during this period. With the Civil War over, Texans returned to find their state in an economic depression. Farms, ranches, and industries were run down and neglected. Confederate money was now useless. The only assets readily available were the Longhorn cattle which, untended during the war years, had

was passed creating six companies of Rangers to be known as the Frontier Battalion, at the same time another company was formed as the Special Force. The Frontier Battalion was raised to serve against the Indians on the Western frontier; the Special Force, commanded by Captain L H McNelly, was given the duty of ridding south Texas of the many Mexican cattle thieves and other outlaws. McNelly carried out his duty with ruthless efficiency. In June, 1875 he intercepted a band of Mexicans driving a herd of stolen cattle. Here is part of his report on the fight:

'The Mexicans then started at a full run, and I found that our horses could not overtake them. So I ordered three of my best mounted men to pass to their right flank and press them so as to force a stand. And as I had anticipated, the Mexicans turned to drive my men off, but [the Rangers] held their ground, and I arrived with four or five men, when the raiders broke. After that it was a succession of single hand fights for six miles before we got the last one. Not one escaped out of the twelve that were driving the cattle. They were all killed. I have never seen men fight with such desperation . . . I lost one man . . . We captured twelve horses, guns, pistols, saddles, and 265 head of beef cattle belonging in the neighborhood of King's Ranch, Santa Gertrudis.'

John Wesley Hardin, credited with killing 40 men, eluded capture until August, 1877 when he was arrested in Florida by Texas Ranger J B Armstrong. On learning Hardin's whereabouts, Armstrong obtained the necessary warrants and permission from local authorities and boarded the train on which the outlaw was travelling with some companions. Armstrong drew his .45 Colt Peacemaker which had a 7½-inch barrel. On seeing this revolver, in particular use with the Rangers, Hardin cried, 'Texas, by God!' and went for his own pistol—but the gun got snagged in his suspenders! One of Hardin's companions sent a bullet through Armstrong's hat and the Ranger promptly shot the man dead. Determined to take Hardin alive, Armstrong grabbed for the killer's gun, but was kicked backward into an empty seat. Armstrong then knocked Hardin unconscious with his Colt. He disarmed the other men and returned to Texas with Hardin, who received a long prison term.

A Texas trail boss leading the herd, as portrayed by Frederic Remington.

A year after Hardin's capture, Ranger Colts took the life of notorious outlaw Sam Bass in a shoot-out at Round Rock, Texas. The Special Force was disbanded in 1881 and the Frontier Battalion in 1901, when the service was reorganized as the Texas Ranger Force to meet the changing requirements of the 20th century. While the Rangers were chasing Indians and bandits, the Texas cowboy was stamping his own brand on American history. The trail-driving years brought these 'weather-beaten rough riders' to the notice of the nation at large. 'With the great annual cattle drives which start from the arid plains of the Red River and the Pecos,' ran an article in Harper's New Monthly Magazine of July 1884, 'comes the wild cow-boy, with his six-shooter on his hip and his leathern [gunbelt] bristling with little metal cylinders.' It has been estimated that from 1866 to 1895 some ten million Longhorns were driven north from the land of the Lone Star flag, giving a special meaning to the couplet:

Other states were made or born,
Texas grew from hide and horn.

The ominous clouds in the background may indicate approaching trouble in *Cattle Drive* by James Walker.

2
THE
TRAIL DRIVES

Over the prairies wide and brown,
On through the wilds where there ain't no town.
Swimming the rivers that bar our way,
Trailing the cattle day after day.
Traditional cowboy song

The Texas Longhorn, fierce and feral, was the bedrock on which the great cattle country of the Southwest was founded. The Longhorns of the trail driving years were incredibly hardy creatures, able to thrive on little sustenance. In appearance they were slab-sided, rawboned and rangy with a thick tough hide, mostly black or dark brown in color. Steers carried a pair of horns with an average spread—tip to tip—from three to five feet. Its beef was not as good as that of corn-fed domestic cattle, but Texas had Longhorns in the millions and the meat fed the factory workers in the cities, the construction crews that built the railroads, the gold and silver miners of the West, and the reservation Indians. Longhorns were also driven to the Northern Plains to stock the vast open ranges there, thus spreading the cattle industry far and wide.

The ancestry of this significant beast can be traced through the black fighting bulls of Spain —descendants of the cattle driven into that country by the Moors—to the extinct auroch forebears of all European cattle. The first domestic cattle to arrive in the New World came with Columbus on his second trip to Santo Domingo in 1493; and the little black cattle were among the livestock of Gregorio de Villalobos when he came to Mexico as Viceroy of New Spain in 1521.

Wherever the Spanish ventured in the New World, cattle went with them. On moving into regions north of the Rio Grande in the late 17th and early 18th centuries they stocked their Missions and *ranchos* with Spanish cattle. Indian raids and the open range encouraged many of these animals to escape into the wild. There they rapidly increased in numbers and developed the characteristics that enabled them to survive and flourish on the arid ranges of the Southwest. The Texas Longhorn evolved from these wandering herds, a distinctly North American breed resulting from natural selection and adaption to environment. In the period between the Texas revolution and the Civil War the wild Longhorns became so numerous that they had little value in the Lone Star State.

Trail driving began in the late 1830s when herds of from 300 to 1000 were gathered in the Nueces and Rio Grande country and driven to markets in the cities of the interior. In 1842 a herd of 1500 was trailed to Missouri; that same year the driving of cattle to New Orleans began. In 1846 Edward Piper drove 1000 head to Ohio. In 1850 drives began to California to get beef to the gold miners who were pouring into the Eldorado state. Six years later came the first drive from Texas to Chicago. These trail drives ended with the outbreak of the Civil War and the Longhorns, untended, proliferated greatly on the ranges. It has been estimated that at the close of the Civil War, 1865, there were five million Longhorns in Texas. And these cattle were almost the only source of revenue in the state.

In Texas, Longhorns were sold as cheaply as three or four dollars a head, and even at that rock-bottom price there were few buyers in the state. In the meat hungry north, whose livestock had been greatly depleted by the demands of the Civil War, Texas cattle could fetch 40 dollars a head. Over the next 25 years some 10 million head were driven northward from the 'Longhorn State,' mostly over the Goodnight-Loving Trail, the Chisholm Trail, and the Western Trail. In 1866 approximately 260,000 Longhorns were driven across the Red River for the northern markets, chiefly over the Shawnee Trail to Sedalia, Missouri, the railhead to St Louis and other cities. But this trail, crossing as it did the domesticated cattle land of southeastern Kansas and Missouri, brought troubles and danger to the Texas drovers. The cause of the problems was the parasite tick carried by the Longhorns that spread the deadly Texas or Spanish fever among the resident northern cattle. The Longhorns were immune to the disease.

The menace was acknowledged by Kansas and Missouri farmers before the outbreak of the Civil War and they had actively opposed the entry of Texas cattle. Now, in 1866, they did so again, with even more vigor. This resentment was compounded by the activity of armed gangs of ruffians and robbers who, under the pretext of guarding the land against the dreaded fever, preyed on the Texas cowboys. 'The southwestern Missouri roads leading to Sedalia were the scenes of the worst work of these outlaws,' wrote Joseph McCoy in his book on the cattle trade published in 1874. 'When outright murder was not resorted to as the readiest means of getting possession of a herd, drovers were flogged until they promised to abandon their stock, mount their horses, and get out of the country as quick as they could.' And once having obtained possession of the cattle, McCoy commented, the robbers seemed to lose all fear of the fever and went on to sell them, pocketing the proceeds themselves.

Faced with this flagrant thieving activity, and with the farmers' and grangers' demands for stricter quarantine legislation, the situation was fast becoming impossible for the Texans who wanted the eastern cities' market. Joseph Mc-Coy provided the solution in 1867 when he es-

Occasionally there was time for entertainment on the trail. Cowboys singing around the campfire in 1910.

Top: After the drive, the cowboys wanted some fun (*In Without Knocking* by Charles M Russell).

Bottom: Loading Texas cattle into railroad cars at a Kansas railhead in the 1870s.

The chuck wagon was one of the most important pieces of equipment on the drive (S Durand painting). Inset: *Cowboy*, painted by Frederic Remington about 1890. Note the 10-gallon hat, the leather chaps and the bandana.

tablished Abilene in Kansas as a trouble-free railhead depot for Texas cattle, and publicized the route pioneered by Jesse Chisholm, a half-breed trader. With its tap roots in Southern Texas, the Chisholm Trail ran north right across central Texas, on through the Indian Territory (Oklahoma) and halfway across Kansas (a region where the quarantine strictures did not apply) to Abilene.

The long trail crossed a number of major rivers, the Colorado, the Brazos, the Red River, the Cimarron, the Canadian and the Arkansas. It was a popular route with the Texans, embracing the best fords and water holes, with plenty of grass for the cattle to feed on. Between 1867 and 1871 some 1½ million Longhorns passed over the Chisholm Trail to Abilene. 'From 200 to 400 yards wide, beaten into the bare earth, it reached over hill and through valley for over 600 miles,' wrote an old time cowboy describing the Chisholm Trail. 'A chocolate band amid the green prairies, uniting the North and the South. As the marching hoofs wore it down and the wind and the waters

washed the earth away, it became lower than the surrounding country.'

Initially, Texas cattle were shipped to the meat plants of the east, via the succeeding railheads in Kansas; later herds were sent to stock, or to fatten on, the rich grasslands of the northern plains. The higher prices Chicago meat companies were willing to pay for cattle fattened on northern ranges increased the northward flow in the 1870s. When Dodge City became the major railhead in Kansas it was serviced by the Western Trail, which also extended to the cattle town of Ogalalla, Nebraska, and into Dakota Territory. It took three months to trek a herd from San Antonio to Abilene, six months from Texas to the northern plains. The Goodnight-Loving Trail struck west through Texas, then swung north through New Mexico, Colorado, and into Wyoming. The trail drive, arduous and unromantic though it was in reality, appealed to many young Texans who yearned for adventure, to see places other than their home range. Jim Herron, in *Going Up the Texal Trail*, describes his joining a trail crew in

Opposite: A few stores were to be found on the trail. Doan's Store was at a crossing of the Red River on the Western Trail.

Above left: Oliver Loving, pioneer of the Goodnight-Loving Trail. Center: W J 'One-armed Jim' Wilson. Right: Nelson Story, the cattleman.

1880 when he was but 14 years old:

'I had always wanted to be a real cowboy. The Western Trail passed close to the range where we held Father's cattle. Many big herds passed that way daily in the summer months. One day a herd came swinging into sight. I learned that this herd was heading for the Black Hills of Dakota ... When I rode up [to the trail boss] I asked, "You need a good man?" The boss stood high in his stirrups and shaded his eyes with one hand, all the while looking across the prairie. "Wheah is this man?" he asked. "I sho' don't see him." The two men with him howled with laughter.' Despite the joshing, Herron was hired and when a veteran cowboy warned him that he ran the risk of getting scalped by Indians, Herron boldly replied, 'I'm bound to be a cowboy, even if I have to be a bald-headed one.'

Open range cattle wandered freely over a wide area in search of forage. Few ranchers had full legal title to the land they called their own; each cattleman claimed a certain region of the plains as his range according to the num-ber of cattle he owned and his priority of use. The ranges were unfenced and cattle from different outfits intermingled, therefore the animals were branded to determine ownership. The spring roundup was the gathering together and sorting of the scattered cattle in preparation for the trail drive north. The cowboys and vaqueros would sweep the wide country, searching for and surrounding the dispersed Longhorns and driving them to a point of concentration. In Texas the roundup was especially difficult, with the cattle concealed in thick brush and cactus country, mesquite and chaparral jungles. To protect his legs from the dagger-like thorns, the Texas cowhand wore leather leggings called *chaparejos*, a Mexican-Spanish word that was shortened to 'chaps.'

The roundup was hard work and required all the cowboy's skills in driving out stubborn, half-wild Longhorns from brush and broken country, and in roping and branding them. Once corralled, the animals were deprived of food and water for several days, by which time they were much subdued and when released they were so preoccupied with the desire to drink that they did not run off into brush. Meanwhile, the mavericks were roped and branded. Unbranded calves kept close to their branded mothers and this signified ownership. Motherless calves or strays were called 'mavericks,' a name believed to have originated from the unbranded cattle owned by Colonel Sam Maverick, a Texas lawyer.

The story goes that in 1845 Maverick accepted a herd of cattle as payment of a debt and that he did little to look after them; the unmarked animals roamed far and wide and other ranchers took to adding this unbranded stock to their own herds. The term 'maverick' for an unbranded beast spread throughout the cattle country. It became a general rule that a cattleman was entitled to appropriate any maverick found on his range. There were, however, many disputes over such unbranded animals. The introduction of barbed wire fences enabled ranchers to keep their cattle separated and ended the need for the old-time open range roundup.

A trail herd of 3,000 head was found to be the most manageable. Usually about ten cowboys,

including the trail boss, or drover, were required to handle such a herd; the trail boss was hired by the cattle owner to drive his herd to market, the drover bought his cattle, driving them to market aided by hired cowhands. The cattle owner provided the horses, maybe six to a man, and the cowboy furnished his own saddle and bedding. The riders changed horses several times a day, for although cow ponies were hardy they would tire after three or four hours of constant activity. The job of looking after the remuda, the string of saddle horses held ready for use, was generally given to a youth learning to be a cowboy.

Cowhands were paid an average 30 dollars a month, the cook usually getting five dollars more. The trail boss, who bore full responsibility for the herd, received about 100 to 125 dollars a month, and probably a bonus at trail's end if he got the cattle to market with little loss. The cook drove the mess or chuckwagon, which carried the food, the bedrolls, and many other items necessary for the long journey. The

Crossing the Red River. A modern re-creation of a Texas longhorn trial drive from San Antonio to Dodge City.

A photograph taken in the 1880s of a cowboy trail boss in Montana fully equipped with lariat, rifle and revolver.

chuckwagon was the focal point of a trail camp. Here the cowboys would eat and relax after the day's work, talk about the day's events, tell stories and sing traditional ditties. The cook was an important man and it did not do to upset him with a careless word or to complain about the chuck he prepared. If you were foolish enough to do so he could make life very unpleasant for you. There is the story of a canny cowboy who broke open a biscuit and said:

'It's burnt on the bottom and the top, it's raw in the middle and salty as hell—just the way I like 'em.'

The cattle were moved at the slow rate of ten to 15 miles a day, in a column about 50 feet wide and strung out nearly a mile long. 'The word "drive" is a misnomer as applied to the trail,' commented an article on the cattle trade in *Harper's New Monthly Magazine* of July 1884. 'It is exactly this which should *not* be done. Cattle . . . headed in the direction of their long journey, should be allowed to "drift" rather than be urged. Walking as they feed, they will accomplish their twelve or fifteen miles a day with but little exertion to themselves, and with very much less care and anxiety on the part of the herder.'

When properly handled the animals soon became accustomed to the trail routine and settled down, a dominant steer taking the lead and usually holding it throughout the trek. Some cattle owners had trained steers to regularly lead the others, such as Charles Goodnight's celebrated 'Old Blue,' who with a bell around his neck headed drives for eight years; when he died Goodnight had his horns mounted in his ranch office. The more active animals would march near the front, the 'drags'—the weak or lazy cattle—in the rear.

Two top hands would ride 'point,' one on ei-

Opposite top: A photograph of a roundup and branding in Arizona in the early 1880s. Bottom: Longhorns on a trail drive heading north from Texas in the 1870s, a detail taken from a painting by the artist Tom Lea.

ther side of the column's head to keep the herd on course, then came the 'swing' riders followed by the 'flank' riders who kept the cattle in line. 'Dragmen' were stationed along the rear sides of the herd to urge on the lagging animals and to prevent them from escaping. Riding drag was the worst job because of the clouds of thick dust kicked up by the herd. The task was usually given to new, inexperienced cowhands. Young Jim Herron, on joining the trail crew, considered himself 'the proudest boy in Texas. We headed north the next morning, me riding drag.' The trail boss or his assistant would ride 15 to 20 miles ahead of the column to scout for water, grass, and a campsite for the night.

'We always tried to reach water before sundown,' recalled Charles Goodnight to J Evetts Haley, in *Charles Goodnight: Cowman and Plainsman.* 'This gave us ample time to have the cattle filled and everything arranged for a pleasant night. The herd was put in a circle, the cattle being a comfortable distance apart. At first, when the cattle were fresh, I used a double guard; that is, half the men guarded the first part of the night, the other half the latter part. In storms or stampedes we were all on duty.'

A stampede, an ever present threat, usually occurred at night. The Longhorn, because of its wildness, was easily alarmed and quick to move. A sudden clap of thunder or other sharp noise, the smell of a wolf, the bark of a coyote, the sound of a rattlesnake, any of a host of things might bring some of the animals swiftly to their feet in fright, the fear would spread and suddenly the herd was running in blind panic. And no cattle can stampede like the Longhorn could; modern cross-breeds do not get scared, or have the ability to run like the wild Texas cattle. Experienced trail drivers held the belief that if a herd could be kept from stampeding in the first week or so on the trail then the danger of one occurring was greatly diminished, the trail slogan being: the best way to handle a stampede is to try and prevent it happening.

'A good herd boss,' J Frank Dobie tells us in

The Longhorns, 'would not bed his cattle on ground that sounded hollow, in a narrow valley, or on a rough point. He picked, if possible, the kind of level ground the cattle would pick for themselves for a bed. He kept the camp quiet and not too far away from the herd. He watered out the cattle thoroughly and saw that they got their fill of grass before lying down.'

The cowhands would sleep near the chuckwagon and its fire, taking turns to guard the cattle, for Longhorns had to be constantly watched throughout the night. Working two-hour shifts, two riders would circle the herd continuously, riding slowly in opposite directions, probably humming, whistling, or crooning in a low voice to reassure the nervous animals. Nearly all the old cowboy songs were

A photograph of a typical Texas longhorn steer.

slow, as slow as a night mount walks around sleeping cattle, and most of them were mournful. Night horses soon learned their duty and if a rider briefly fell asleep in the saddle the horse could be relied on to continue its leisurely pace. The cowboy often sang of his affinity with his horse. *I Ride an Old Paint* (a pinto) was a traditional song, a chorus of which went as follows:

Oh when I die, take my saddle off the wall,
Put it on my pony, lead him from his stall.
Tie my bones to his back, turn our faces to
  the West,
And we'll ride the prairies that we love the
  best.

Cowboys dreaded a stampede (from the Spanish *estampida*) chiefly because of the time and effort involved in reassembling the scattered herd. A stampede always resulted in the loss of some animals, and injuries inflicted on each other with their horns. And running for miles 'worked the tallow off them,' adversely affecting their market weight. Jim Herron recalled the dread of the stampede and the technique called 'milling' employed to bring the rushing beasts to a halt.

'Stampedes were something frightful to see, and any man's knees will rattle when the big Longhorns start to run. There was nothing to do then but run with them, stay ahead of them if

Cowboy in a Stampede by Frederic Remington.

you could, and turn them into a tight mill when you got the chance, circle them until they was wound up as tight as an eight-day clock on Sunday. It took the best night horse to stay with them. Once, we rode alongside the leaders for five miles, then gathered cattle over that five-mile stretch all the next day.'

An' woe to the rider and woe to the steed,
That falls in front of the mad stampede.

It appears, however, that few cowboys were actually trampled to death in stampedes. Ab

Blocker, veteran Texas trail boss, said that he 'never heard of a cowboy being run over in a stampede.' He maintained, as did others, that stampeding cattle, no matter how dark the night, would split and go around a man in front of them. It is said that more cowboys were killed by lightning than maddened steers. But it took courage to ride out a stampede on a black night over country full of gopher holes or prairie-dog burrows. Many a horse threw its rider after stepping into such a hole.

'What need to tell of the miseries of that dreadful night,' wrote drover and former Texas Ranger R H Williams of a stampede in the 1860s. 'The wind and the rain buffeted and soaked us; the thunder rolled overhead almost incessantly, and the cattle became wilder and more terrified the more we tried to stay their headlong flight. Fortunately for me the country was open, rolling prairie for miles and miles; had it been brushy I should probably have lost the whole drove, at least temporarily. As it was when day at last broke, and we rounded up the cattle about twelve miles from camp, forty of them had disappeared.'

Rattlesnakes and scorpions were other, if minor, hazards of the trail drive and range life. Experienced cowboys always shook their boots out before pulling them on in case a scorpion might be lurking inside. A scorpion sting would not kill a man but it would cause him much pain. Rattlesnakes prefer dry regions and are mostly found in the southwest. All rattlesnakes —of which there are thirty species—are venom-ous but some are more dangerous to humans than others—the most deadly species being the western diamondback, the timber and the Mojave rattlesnakes. The bigger the snake the more lethal it is, because size determines its striking distance and the quality and quantity of its venom. When alarmed, or ready to strike, it vibrates its tail rattle, then lunges forward with its jaws open to the fullest extent, driving its long curved fangs deep into its victim, in-jecting venom through the hollow fangs. The venom can kill a man. The biggest rattler is the western diamondback, found from Texas to California, which grows to a length of some six feet.

The Texas cowboy learned from the Mexican *vaquero* that the poison of the Spanish dagger, a type of thorny plant, jabbed into the flesh near a rattlesnake bite, could neutralize the venom. Cowboys (who often wore snake skin bands around their hats) would either shoot rattlers or kill them with their quirts, or short whips. 'I generally killed them with my quirt,' a cowboy recalled in Thayer's *Marvels of the New West*, 1888, 'which is about 18 inches long, made of rawhide and leather plaited together, with a piece of iron in the handle. A snake can-not strike unless it first coils itself up, so you can hit it when it is gliding off, with even a short weapon, without fear of the conse-quences . . . One of my horses was once bitten

A Frederic Remington illustration of several cowboys and their horses struggling to pull a chuckwagon out of the mire.

right on the nose. His head swelled up tremendously and he could not eat for two or three days, but he ultimately recovered. When a man gets bitten, the cure chiefly relied on is copious doses of whiskey.'

Crossing a deep, wide river was always a difficult operation fraught with peril, only possible if the cattle had leaders to brave the way first. Once the Longhorns had taken the plunge they were good swimmers. Normally a cowboy would swim his horse ahead of the herd as an example. Having got the herd into the river and swimming for the opposite bank, there was always the danger of them stampeding in the water. A strange sound, a floating log or other flotsom, even a sudden eddy might spook the leading animals to turn about and suddenly the entire herd would be mixed up madly in the water. And the cowhands, risking life and limb, would have to untangle the terrified beasts and get them swimming together in the right direction. A number of cowboys were drowned in river crossings.

Dudley Snyder, of the famous Snyder brothers' cattle company, was noted for training two work oxen as lead swimmers. He would unyoke them at a stream and they would head the herd across. They never faltered in their duty, not even when faced with the intimidating expanse of the Mississippi (crossed on a drive during the Civil War), and the herd always followed them. Snyder kept secret his method of training his swimming oxen and, apparently, no other trail driver of later years managed to emulate the feat. The chuckwagon was either floated across with logs lashed to its wheels, or emptied and pulled across by ropes, the contents being rafted over.

The Red River was just one of ten rivers on the Chisholm Trail. But it had a special significance because it marked the boundary between Texas and the Indian Territory, the land reserved for Indian tribes removed from other states by the U S Government, that eventually formed part of Oklahoma when that state was created in 1907. In its low condition the sluggish river could be crossed at many points, the most popular place being Red River Station, where a shelving sandbar ran out from the northern bank and made it possible for cattle to walk across the river. On the Western Trail,

Doan's Crossing was a favored spot; it was named after C F Doan who opened a store there to service the trail crews.

The ruthless destruction of the buffalo—which had once roamed the western prairies in their millions—by professional white hunters deprived the Indians of their chief means of sustenance. The well-ordered society of the Plains tribes was largely dependent on the all-providing buffalo, which gave the Indians meat, skins for tents and clothes, and horns and bones for weapons and tools. The Indians used every part of the beast, nothing was wasted. The white hunters, on the other hand, wiped out the great herds for the commercial value of their hides, leaving the meat to rot on the plains.

It was easy to shoot a buffalo from a safe distance. An experienced hunter could kill animals faster than a good skinner could remove the hides; hunters often killed 250 buffalo a day and many slaughtered up to 3000 a year. Having exterminated the southern herd, the professional hunters turned to the northern herd and, between 1876 and 1883, destroyed that also. The US military approved the mass slaughter as a means of depriving the troublesome Plains Indians of their staff of life, thus making it easy to subdue them. Cattlemen were also thankful that the swarming buffalo had been removed from the open ranges to make way for the growing population of beef livestock.

The tribes of the Indian Territory, wise to the laws of the white man, demanded a toll of ten cents a head on all cattle trailed through their land. The Texans grudgingly paid the tax or gave cattle in lieu of payment. The Indians, many of whom raised cattle themselves, also demanded the right to inspect the herds to see if any of their own animals had got mixed with the passing Longhorns. Some Texans refused to comply with the Indian demands and endeavored to strong-arm their way through. John Wesley Hardin, young trail boss and gunfighter, had a run-in with Osage braves on the Chisholm Trail in 1871. While he was absent from the camp the Osages had paid a visit; scaring

Opposite top: A photograph of a cattle drive from New Mexico to Kansas taken in the 1880s by F M Steel. Bottom: A group of cowboys of the 1880s preparing to take their turns at standing night guard over the herd.

the cook and some cowhands, they cut out a few cattle and departed, taking with them Hardin's prized silver bridle. So when a band of 20 warriors returned to take some more cattle, Hardin rode up to a big Indian riding a pony wearing the Texan's fancy bridle.

'I asked him how much he would take for it,' wrote Hardin in his autobiography, 'and offered him five dollars. He grunted an assent and gave me the bridle. When I got it, I told him that [it] was my bridle and someone had stolen it from camp that morning. He frowned and grunted and started to get the bridle back . . . I jabbed him with my pistol and when this would not stop him, I struck him over the head with it. He fell back and yelled to his companions. This put the devil in them. They came up in a body and demanded cattle again. I told them "no" as I had done before. An Indian rode to the herd and cut out a big beef steer. I told him to get out of the herd and pulled my pistol to emphasize my remarks. He was armed and drew his, saying that if I did not let him cut the beef out, he would kill the animal. I told him that if he killed the animal, I would kill him. Well, he killed the beef and I killed him. The other Indians promptly vanished. If they had not, there would have been more dead Indians.'

The ferocious Comanches of Texas were not so easily dealt with as were the subdued tribes of the Indian Territory. For nearly 200 years they had waged war against the Spaniards in Mexico, and they became bitter enemies of the Texans who had taken their best hunting grounds and fought them relentlessly for almost forty years. The Comanches plagued the Goodnight-Loving Trail that ran west through Texas, then north into New Mexico and Colorado. The Indian raiders sometimes managed to run off whole herds. In July, 1867 a war party of Comanches attacked Oliver Loving, trail-driving partner of Charles Goodnight, while he was riding far ahead of the herd.

With the whooping warriors chasing them, Loving and his cowboy companion, one-armed Bill Wilson, raced for the Pecos River, where they took up a defensive position in the tall canebreaks. They managed to hold off the Indians but Loving was hit by a bullet in the wrist and the side. When darkness fell, Loving, convinced he was dying, implored Wilson to save himself. Wilson reluctantly agreed, on the understanding that he would find help and return for his injured boss. Stripping to his underwear, the one-armed cowboy floated downriver, out of reach of the besieging Comanches. The bootless Wilson walked for several days until he met up with Goodnight and the herd. When a rescue party reached the place where Loving had been hiding, he could not be found.

Two weeks later Goodnight learned that his wounded partner had dragged himself five miles away, where he was picked up by Mexicans and taken to Fort Sumner, New Mexico. When Goodnight arrived at the fort he found Loving on the way to recovery, but soon after an infection of the wound proved fatal. Goodnight thought highly of his dead partner and friend and the next year gave his widow 40,000 dollars, half of the profit he had cleared on the cattle deals. The fierce Comanches were not subdued until 1874 when the military mounted a determined campaign against them.

Nelson Story drove his herd through country thick with hostile Sioux on a marathon drive of 1500 miles that took six months to complete. After making some money in the gold fields of Montana, Story decided to invest his capital in

Below left: *Taking the Robe,* a painting by Frederic Remington. Right: *Fight for the Waterhole* by the same artist.

A scene of a roundup after a sketch by Frenzeny and Tavernier in *Harper's Weekly* of 2 May 1874.

cattle. Having purchased 1000 Longhorns at Fort Worth, Texas, he trailed them with hired hands to Missouri, where he was stopped by the human barrier of armed farmers and grangers. Instead of trying to force or buy his way through to Sedalia, Story determined to drive his herd all the way to Montana where he knew he could sell the beeves to the gold miners at a high profit.

He headed the cattle west, then swung north and veered east to reach Fort Leavenworth, where he purchased wagons and oxen to pull them, and hired bull whackers to handle the teams. He loaded the wagons with stores and provisions and, together with the cattle, rolled west along the Oregon Trail to Fort Laramie, Wyoming, where he learned that the Sioux were on the warpath and that it would be highly dangerous to continue through the Powder River country. Nevertheless, Story was fixed on reaching Montana. He armed his twenty-seven men with the latest Remington breech-loaded, rapid-fire rifles and headed north.

Near Fort Reno, Story's caravan was pounced upon by a party of Sioux. They wounded two cowboys with arrows and ran off part of the herd. Story and his men followed the Indians, and when the redskins made camp, the cowboys hit them hard and fast with the new rifles and got back all the cattle. Story pressed on to Fort Phil Kearny, in what is now northern Wyoming. Here, the post commander, Colonel Carrington, told Story that to proceed through Sioux country would mean certain death for him and his crew. He ordered Story to halt near the fort and wait for permission to continue. The cowboys had to corral the cattle several miles from the fort because the soldiers required all the grass near the fort for their own animals.

Story was in a most unfavorable situation. If the Indians attacked his caravan in force the soldiers were too far away to give any assistance. And if he delayed his journey too long the snows would completely close the trail. That would entail wintering at the fort and selling his cattle cheaply to the soldiers. He decided to take his chances on the trail and his men agreed with him. At night, the wagons and cattle managed to pass the fort without being detected. Attacked several times by small bands of Sioux, the party fought them off, thanks to their rapid-firing Remingtons, and suffered only one death, a hunter riding ahead of the caravan, who was captured by the Indians, scalped and 'pincushioned' with arrows.

Six weeks after pushing on from Fort Phil Kearny, the caravan arrived at its destination, Virginia City, on 9 December 1866, where eager buyers snapped up the provisions and the cattle, paying 100 dollars a head for the Longhorns that Nelson Story had purchased for 10 dollars a head.

Dodge City, Kansas, in the 1880s. The sign in the foreground informs visiting cowboys that 'The Carrying of Fire Arms' is 'Strictly Prohibited.'

3
THE CATTLE TOWNS

We all hit town and we hit her on the fly,
We bedded down the cattle on a hill close by.
We rounded 'em up and put 'em on the cars,
And that was the last of the old Two Bars.

The Old Chisholm Trail, cowboy song

On completion of the trail drive, the cattle sales were concluded, and the animals were penned and loaded into the railroad cars. The cowhands collected their hard-earned pay and cut loose in the town. Having endured the rigors, the monotony and deprivations of the long ride, the young cowboy, dirty and dry, with about 100 dollars burning a hole in his pocket, was primed to blow the lot on a wild spree of drinking, dancing, whoring and gambling. And the opportunists and entrepreneurs attracted to the cowtowns provided ample facilities to cater to the cowboy's simple needs.

The Kansas cattle towns of Abilene, Ellsworth, Newton and Wichita all enjoyed a brief period of rip-roaring celebrity. Dodge City, 'Queen of the Cowtowns,' spawned history and legend for ten hectic years, 1875-85. And the law officers who managed to keep the peace in these anarchic boom towns have, over the years, attained the status of folk heroes. These violent, licentious railhead towns gave real meaning to the appellation 'Wild West.' Dressed in their flamboyant finery, toting their revolv-

ers, the cowboys invaded the town intent on showing off and having a good time. After a visit to a barbershop, then perhaps to a photographer's studio to have souvenir pictures taken with their trail buddies, the Texans flung themselves into the fleshpots with amazing exultation.

'The cowboy enters the dance with a peculiar zest,' wrote Joseph McCoy, pioneer promoter of Abilene, 'not stopping to divest himself of his sombrero, spurs, or pistols, but just as he dismounts from his cow-pony so he goes into the dance . . . his huge spurs jingling at every step or motion; his revolvers flapping up and down . . . his eyes lit up with excitement and liquor, he plunges in and "hoes it down" at a terrible rate, in the most approved yet awkward country style, often swinging his "partner" clean off the floor.'

Abilene was the first of the famous Kansas cattle towns and it set the pattern for the others

One of the most popular places to relax was the saloon. These cowboys of the 1890s are drinking in a Texas bar.

that followed. It served as a busy, bellowing shipping point from where, during the period 1867 to 1872, some 1½ million Longhorns were sent by railroad to the Kansas City and Chicago meat dressing plants. First settled in 1856, Abilene remained a quiet hamlet of a dozen cabins until 1867 when Illinois cattle dealer Joseph McCoy decided that the place would make the ideal site for a cattle terminus (the railroad had reached Abilene that year). McCoy had heard about the difficulties encountered by the Texas drovers trailing to the railhead at Sedalia, Missouri; the cowboys had been plagued by cattle thieves and attacked by angry farmers, the latter intent on turning back the herds for fear that the Longhorns would bring the dreaded Texas or Mexican cattle fever.

McCoy observed that another trail and another railhead were required, an isolated spot away from the sensitive populated regions. 'Abilene was selected,' he explains in his *Historic Sketches of the Cattle Trade of the West and Southwest*, 1874, 'because the country was entirely unsettled, well watered, had excellent

Games of chance were also popular. These trail hands are playing faro in Morenci, Arizona Territory in 1895.

grass, and nearly the entire area of country was adapted to holding cattle. And it was the farthest point east at which a good depot for cattle business could have been made.'

He bought 250 acres on the edge of the settlement, built the three-story Drover's Cottage hotel, erected cattle pens, loading chutes, barns and livery stables. When all was ready, McCoy sent word to the cattlemen and buyers that Abilene was the place to meet and do business in safety. He publicized the route pioneered by the old halfbreed trader Jesse Chisholm, and the Chisholm Trail became the main cattle route from Texas to Kansas. That first year Abilene received 35,000 cattle, 75,000 in 1868, 350,000 in 1869, 300,000 in 1870, and 700,000 in 1871.

The town quickly became notorious for its lawlessness and vice. 'I have seen many fast towns,' commented John Wesley Hardin, cowboy and gunfighter, 'but I think Abilene beats

Left, top to bottom: Luke Short, the gambler and dangerous gunman; 'Rowdy Joe' Lowe, the saloon keeper and gunfighter; Bat Masterson, the marshal of Dodge City; James Butler 'Wild Bill' Hickok when he was marshal of Abilene, Kansas; Tom Smith—one-time marshall of Abilene. Above right: The famous Long Branch Saloon in Dodge City. Below right: Wichita in the 1870s.

them all. The town was filled with sporting men and women, gamblers, cowboys, desperadoes and the like. It was well-supplied with bar rooms, hotels, barber shops and gambling houses, and everything was open.' Abilene was divided by the railroad into two sections: the north side of the track housed the respectable element, the churches, banks, newspaper office and several large stores. The south side accommodated the hotels, saloons and gambling dens. 'When you are on the north side,' stated the Topeka *Kansas State Record*, describing Abilene in 1871, 'you are in Kansas, and hear sober and profitable conversation on the subject of the weather, the price of land and the crops; when you cross to the south side you are in "Texas," and talk about cattle . . . five at least out of every ten [men you meet] are Texans.'

The lads from the Lone Star State were a wild and whooping lot indeed, who delighted in charging up and down the boardwalks on their ponies, barging into saloon and dance hall, shooting out the lights, and using their guns on anybody daring or foolish enough to oppose their belligerent antics. Clearly, something had to be done to contain and control these Texas terrors who, if not restrained, might eventually dominate the entire township. A marshal was needed, but he would have to be a very brave and able man. Theodore C Henry, Abilene's first mayor, made the right choice in 'Bear River' Tom Smith.

Smith was unusual in that he preferred to use his fists instead of guns to subdue a troublemaker. And he could use his fists with remarkable ability. Cowboys and frontiersmen did not resort to fisticuffs to settle an argument—a gun or knife concluded the difference once and for all. The new marshal's flying fists came as a jolting and sobering surprise to the swaggering Texans. Hardly anything is known about Smith before his years out West. It is said that he hailed from New York where he was a prize

fighter and later a member of the police force. This would certainly account for his fistic ability. In 1868 he established a reputation as a peace officer at Bear River, Wyoming, one of the 'hell-on-wheels' towns that followed the construction gangs of the Union Pacific Railroad. Henceforth he was known as 'Bear River' Tom Smith.

He became Abilene's chief of police on 4 June 1870. A broad-shouldered middleweight, nearly six feet tall, he was never known to back away from trouble. He immediately began to enforce the town's ordinance that forbade the carrying of firearms—a sensitive point with gun-proud Texans. Smith knocked down a lot of cowboys who, on being asked calmly and politely to give up their guns, refused to comply. Tom socked them hard and took their weapons.

On one occasion, on hearing shots from a saloon, he went to investigate. He walked through the only door and there at the far end of the narrow room was a drunken Texan brandishing his pistol. As Tom walked toward the man he noticed that other cowboys had crowded in front of the door, cutting off his exit. He did not

hesitate in his action. Confronting the drunk, he drew his Colt and smashed it over the man's head, knocking him senseless. Stunned for a moment at the lawman's audacity, the other Texans pulled their shooting irons. Tom picked up the unconscious man, slung him over his shoulder and walked out; the cowboys would not shoot for fear of hitting their comrade.

Tom Smith managed to tame the Texans, who came to admire and respect the resolute peace officer who did not kill cowboys. The Abilene *Chronicle* of 8 September 1870 reported that 'The respectable citizens of Abilene may well feel proud of the order and quietness now prevailing in the town . . . Chief of Police T J Smith and his assistants . . . deserve the thanks of the people for the faithful and prompt manner in which they have discharged their official duties.' Sad to relate, the valiant Smith was killed while making an arrest in November 1870, murdered not by wild Texans but by two settlers outside the town's limits. The men were later captured and sentenced to long terms of imprisonment. 'Although our people will never again permit the lawlessness which existed prior to

Faro Players by W L Dodge. This scene in a smoky saloon shows the dealer in his top hat with his Derringer revolver on the table and the cowboys with their holstered guns.

his [Smith's] coming to town,' the *Chronicle* commented, 'yet it will be a long time before his equal will be found in all the essentials required to make a model police officer.'

The man chosen to replace Smith was James Butler 'Wild Bill' Hickok, a lawman of the gunfighter type, born in 1837 in Illinois. An impressive figure, over six feet tall, with shoulder-length hair, he wore fashionable city clothes and always carried two Colt revolvers stuck into a belt or silk sash. He was a marksman, cool and courageous in a dangerous situation, having previously killed a number of men in shoot-outs. His career out West had included jobs as a stagecoach and freight driver; he served the Union Army in the Civil War as a scout, wagonmaster, and spy. He is said to have won his famous sobriquet 'Wild Bill' by stopping a mob, single handed, from lynching a man. He gained fame when an account of his exploits, based on an interview with Colonel George Ward Nichols, was published in *Harper's New Monthly Magazine* of February, 1867.

Hickok was sworn in as marshal of Abilene on 15 April 1871 at a salary of 150 dollars a month. Wild Bill was a man who trod carefully, his eyes alert for any hostile move, and he never took chances. 'He *slid* into a room,' recalled an old-timer, 'keeping his back to the wall, watching the whole crowd like a hawk. He looked like a man who lived in expectation of getting killed.'

Texas cowboy Brown Paschal recalled his first impression of Hickok. 'He came out of Ben Thompson's Bull's Head saloon. He wore a low-crowned, wide black hat and a frock coat. His hair was yellow and it hung down to his shoulders . . . He was standing there with his back to the wall, his thumbs hooked in his red sash. He stood there and rolled his head from side to side looking at everything and everybody . . . just like a mad old bull. I decided then and there that I didn't want any part of him.'

Wild Bill's reputation helped keep the peace in Abilene. While marshal there he was involved in only one recorded shooting incident.

On 5 October 1871 Hickok was having a drink with his friend Mike Williams in the Novelty Bar when he heard a shot in the street. Telling Williams to stay put, Hickok went to investigate, and outside the Alamo saloon confronted a crowd of armed cowboys headed by Phil Coe, a tall Texan gambler and co-owner of the Bull's Head. Coe told the marshal that he had fired at a dog. There was bad blood between Hickok and Coe; Hickok had been told that Coe intended to kill him. Wild Bill ordered the Tex-

ans to give up their guns. Coe pointed his pistol at Hickok.

'Quick as thought,' reported the *Chronicle*, 'the Marshal drew two revolvers and both men fired almost simultaneously.' At that precise moment someone rushed between Hickok and Coe and stopped the marshal's bullets. Coe fired twice, one passing between Wild Bill's legs, the other piercing his coat tail. Hickok fired both guns again, hitting Coe in the stomach and dropping him. Bill covered the other

Texans, saying: 'If any of you want the balance of these pills, come and get them!' There were no takers, and Bill added: 'Now all you mount your ponies and ride for camp, and do it damn quick!' Then Hickok found to his horror that the man who had run between him and Coe at the moment of shooting was Mike Williams, who had come to aid the marshal. Coe died after several days of agony.

With the end of the cattle season, the Abilene city council decided to dispense with the ex-

After driving their herd to Montana, these Texans of the XIT outfit relaxed and had their picture taken in Miles City.

pensive services of Hickok and in December, 1871 appointed J A Gauthie as marshal at 50 dollars a month. Now that their town was firmly established, the good citizens of Abilene decided they could do without the troublesome Texas cattle trade, no matter how lucrative it might be, and in February, 1872 notice was served on the Texas cattlemen 'to seek some other point for shipment, as the inhabitants of Dickinson [County] will no longer submit to the evils of the trade.'

Ellsworth, another railhead on the Kansas Pacific Railway, served as a major cattle town from 1871 to 1873 and, like all places of its kind, it gained a fierce reputation. Laid out in the spring of 1867, the town boasted the biggest stockyards in Kansas, and the only solid sidewalk—made of limestone rock—west of Kansas City in the plains country; the sidewalk was 12 feet wide and ran the length of the Grand Central Hotel, favored house of the top cattlemen. To the east of the town stood the community of Nauchville, the red light district.

Among the gamblers and other social parasites who came to Ellsworth to profit from the

officers were not always chosen for their integrity, but often for their gunfighting ability), and was shot dead in San Antonio in 1884 over a gambling feud.

Gambling was the cowboy's—and the frontiersman's—chief means of recreation. It provided company, excitement and the chance to win a big stake. Card games were the most popular and these included seven-up, blackjack, monte, poker, and faro, the latter known out West as 'bucking the tiger'; William 'Bucky' O'Neill, noted sheriff of Yavapai County, Arizona in the 1880s, won his nickname because of his addiction to faro. Wild Bill Hickok, Bat Masterson, and Wyatt Earp were inveterate gamblers. Hickok was killed—shot in the back—while playing poker, and the five cards that he held at the time included the ace of spades, ace of clubs, eight of clubs, eight of spades, and these 'aces and eights' became known to poker players as the 'Dead Man's Hand.'

Every cattle town and frontier settlement had its gambling houses. Gambling was, to quote Bat Masterson, 'not only the principal and best-paying industry of the town, but was also reckoned among its most respectable.' Professional gamblers who drifted from town to town included Ben Thompson, John Henry 'Doc' Holliday, and Luke Short, all of them skilled in the use of firearms. Luke Short was born in Mississippi and grew up in Texas. As a working cowhand he trailed a herd up to Kansas and became fascinated by the gambling action at Abilene. Preferring poker to poking cows he became a professional gaming man. A small, dapper figure he was, like Doc Holliday, deadly with a gun. Luke carried his short-barreled .45 Colt in a special leather-lined pocket designed so that it did not spoil the hang of his elegant frock coat.

Unlike Holliday, who had a quick temper, cool hand Luke had a long fuse. When a braggart named Brown leaned over the faro table and moved Luke's chips, saying, 'Play it that way, Shorty,' the little gambler let it pass. When Brown repeated his interference Luke warned him to stay away. The troublemaker stepped back, cursing, and went for his gun. But Luke was faster and shot him. Charlie Storms, another professional gambler, once threw chips into Luke's face over a losing turn

free-spending Texans was the celebrated Ben Thompson, a gunfighter credited with 32 killings. British-born Thompson was co-owner with Phil Coe of the Bull's Head saloon in Abilene; when Coe was killed by Hickok, Ben was out of town. At Ellsworth, Ben was joined by his hare-brained brother Billy, who caused a lot of trouble in the town. When Billy's drunken gunplay brought Sheriff Chauncey Whitney to the scene, Billy mortally wounded him with a shotgun blast. Ben held off the enraged onlookers while Billy rode out of town. He was brought to trial in 1877 and acquitted. Ben was later elected marshal of Austin, Texas (peace

To the cowboys, the bartender in the saloon of a western town was one of the more important citizens. This rough and ready barkeeper was painted by Olaf C Seltzer.

of the cards. Storms was the worse for drink and again Luke let the incident pass. Some years later, however, when Storms ran into Short in Tombstone, Arizona, he attempted to shoot him at close range but, according to eyewitness Bat Masterson, 'he was too slow. He got his pistol out, but Luke stuck the muzzle of his own pistol against Storms' heart and pulled the trigger . . . and as he was falling, Luke shot him again. Storms was dead when he hit the ground.'

Newton followed the pattern of the other Kansas cattle towns. Founded in March, 1871 it became a terminus of the Chisholm Trail when the Atchison, Topeka and Santa Fe Railroad reached the town in July that year. By the end of 1871 some 30,000 head of cattle had been shipped out of the place. Newton flourished under the usual clouds of Texan gunsmoke. Cal Johnston, a long-time resident of the town, recalled that the shooting 'was so continuous that it reminded me of a Fourth of July celebration from daylight to midnight. There was shooting when I got up and when I went to bed.' Newton's brothel district was known as 'Hide Park.'

When policeman Mike McCluskie shot a Texan during a quarrel, the killing triggered the shoot-out known as 'Newton's General Massacre.' It took place in the early hours of Sunday, 20 August 1871. A group of cowboy friends of the dead Texan confronted McCluskie in a dance hall. And according to a report in The Kansas Daily Commonwealth, one of them said to McCluskie: 'You are a cowardly son of a bitch! I will blow the top of your head off!' And promptly shot the policeman in the neck, and when he fell, shot him again in the back. Then it seemed that everybody in the crowded place started shooting. When the gunfire ended, nine bodies littered the blood-spattered dance hall. McCluskie and four others died, the rest were injured.

The Commonwealth called it the 'most terrible tragedy that has ever occurred in Kansas during civil times. It is a burning shame and disgrace to Kansas, and measures should be at once adopted to prevent a repetition.' The paper went on to say that as the town's authorities could not keep the peace, the army should be called in and martial law declared. The violence went on. Lawmen came and went with little result. The town continued to disgrace Kansas until 1873, when the railroad reached

Above: *Drifters* by Charles M Russell captures the loneliness of the life.

Below: A bronco-busting scene painted by Frederic Remington, *Turn Him Loose, Bill.*

Above: Cattle arriving at Dodge City, Kansas. Left: An illustration by Frederic Remington showing a gunfight in a saloon. Below left: Dance hall girls were always ready to help the trail hands enjoy themselves. Here are Texas cowboys in Dodge City. Below right: Some cowboys overdid things at the end of a trail drive. This is an example of a cowboy fun in a Kansas cowtown.

Wichita, which supplanted 'Shootin' Newton' as a cattle and trouble center.

Wichita held the dubious distinction of being the roughest, toughest cowtown in Kansas for two years, 1873 and 1874. Like other cattle towns it had its good and bad sections. The bad or cowboy section was called Delano, or West Wichita, situated on the opposite bank of the Arkansas from Wichita proper. City authority did not extend beyond the river and therefore Delano was lawless. 'Rowdy Joe' Lowe, who with his wife 'Rowdy Kate,' ran a dance hall-saloon-brothel in Delano, was stalwart enough to act as his own policeman. If a customer started trouble, Rowdy Joe would promptly knock the nonsense out of him. He had owned similar establishments in Ellsworth and Newton.

'His dance hall [in Delano] is patronized mainly by cattle herders, though all classes visit it; the respectable mostly from curiosity,' reported the *Commonwealth*. 'The Texan, with mammoth spurs on his boots . . . and broad-brimmed sombrero on his head, is seen dancing by the side of a well-dressed, gentlemanly-appearing stranger from some eastern city; both having painted and jeweled courtesans for partners. In the corner of the hall are seen gamblers playing at their favorite game of poker.' A rival establishment was run by E T 'Red' Beard, who sported shoulder-length red hair.

On 3 June 1873 an argument erupted in Red Beard's place between a soldier of the Sixth Cavalry and a woman of the house over a matter of five dollars. The soldier drew his gun and shot the lady through the thigh. Red Beard reacted like the gentleman he was. 'As soon as the shot was fired,' related the *Commonwealth*, 'Red instantly drew his self-cocking revolver and commenced an indiscriminate fusilade, shooting two soldiers . . . The soldiers who were shot [and wounded] were not engaged in the quarrel, and are spoken of by their comrades as being very quiet and gentlemanly. The soldier who commenced the affray escaped unhurt and deserted [his regiment] last night.' A few days later the comrades of the wounded soldiers marched in force on Red Beard's dance hall and set fire to it.

The rivalry between Red and Rowdy Joe exploded into a shoot-out in October 1873; Rowdy Joe

was wounded in the neck and Red in the arm and hip. Beard died of his wounds. Rowdy Joe was later shot dead.

By 1874 Wichita was the leading cattle shipping center, with 200,000 cattle and 2,000 cowboys flooding into the area at the height of the season. The Wichita *Eagle* of 28 May 1874 commented that though 'the cattle season has not yet fully set in . . . there is a rush of gamblers and harlots who are lying in wait for the [cowboy] game which will soon begin to come up from the south.' Wyatt Earp was appointed policeman on the Wichita force in April 1875 but never became marshal. In May 1876 Earp joined the police force of Dodge City, which replaced Wichita as the premier cattle town in 1875 and reigned as 'Queen of the Cowtowns' for ten flamboyant years.

Founded in 1872 some five miles west of Fort Dodge, the army post built in 1864, Dodge City was originally a buffalo hunters' town. With millions of buffalo within hunting range, some 1½ million hides were shipped east from Dodge on the Atchison, Topeka and Santa Fe Railroad. In its early years as the 'Cowboy Capital,' Dodge City was noted for its licentiousness and violence. There is the apocryphal story of the young cowboy who, after a rough night at Newton, got on the train. 'Where do you want to go?' asked the conductor.

'To Hell, I guess,' replied the surly cowboy.

'Well, give me two dollars 50 and get off at Dodge.'

When law and order was established in this turbulent town, its peace officers were celebrated for their excellence, in particular the three redoubtable Masterson brothers, Edward, James, and Bartholomew, the latter better known as 'Bat.' It soon proved to be a town the Texans could not take over and run to suit themselves. 'Don't ever get the impression that you can ride your horses into a saloon, or shoot out the lights in Dodge,' the veteran trail driver advised the young cowhands in Andy Adams' *The Log of a Cowboy*, 1903. 'It may go somewhere else, but it don't go there. So I want to warn you to behave yourselves. You can wear your six-shooters into town, but you'd better leave them at the first place you stop . . . And when you leave town . . . don't ride out shooting . . . for your six-shooters are no match for Winchesters and

Left: *Gunfight* **by Charles M Russell. Above: The shiny brass star of a United States Deputy Marshal in Oklahoma.**

buckshot; and Dodge's [peace] officers are as game a set of men as ever faced danger.'

Edward J. Masterson, eldest of the brothers, was appointed assistant marshal in June, 1877. The Dodge City *Times* remarked that 'He is not very large, but there are not many men who would be anxious to tackle him a second time. He makes a good officer.' In attempting to stop a man named Bob Shaw from killing 'Texas Dick' Moore, Masterson was shot and wounded by Shaw. As Ed fell he returned the fire and hit Shaw in the arm and leg, putting him out of action. Both men recovered and Shaw left Dodge, never to return. Ed Masterson did his duty with distinction and in December, 1877 was promoted to marshal.

On 9 April 1878 Ed disarmed a drunken cowboy named Jack Wagner and handed the sixgun to Wagner's trail boss, Alfred Walker, for safe keeping. A little later, in company with deputy marshal Hayward, Masterson met Wagner again on the sidewalk and saw that he was wearing a gun. Ed went to take possession of the weapon. As Hayward stepped in to assist his chief in the struggle, other Texans stopped him at gunpoint. Wagner fired his revolver into Masterson's stomach, being so close that the discharge flash set the marshal's clothes on fire.

Despite his fatal wound, Ed managed to draw his own gun and shoot Wagner, and also Walker, who had entered the fight. Masterson stumbled into Hoover's saloon and said to the bartender, 'George, I'm shot,' then sank to the floor, his clothes still burning. Ed died 30 minutes later. Meanwhile, Wagner had staggered into another saloon and collapsed; he died the next day. Walker, wounded in the lung and right arm, recovered and returned to Texas. 'The death of Marshal Masterson caused great feeling in Dodge City,' reported the Dodge City *Times*. 'The business houses were draped in mourning and business on Wednesday generally suspended. Elsewhere we give expression of sympathy and ceremonies following this terrible tragedy.'

In June 1878 Jim Masterson, youngest of the brothers, joined the Dodge City police department, of which Wyatt Earp was assistant mar-

shots. Kenedy was seen galloping out of town and a posse was soon after him.

The posse consisted of Bat Masterson, then serving as sheriff of Ford County; his deputy Bill Duffy; Charles Bassett, marshal of Dodge; Wyatt Earp and Bill Tilghman, 'as intrepid a posse as ever pulled a trigger,' commented the Dodge City *Times*. After a long ride they caught up with Kenedy, who was armed with a brace of pistols, a carbine, and a Bowie knife, and brought him back to Dodge in a wounded condition. At his examination before Judge Cook, Kenedy was acquitted for lack of evidence; that is to say, nobody actually saw him fire the shots. Dora Hand was given a fine funeral and

shal. Jim served as marshal from 1879 to 1881. He and Earp were on duty the night Dora Hand was shot. James Kenedy, cowboy son of a wealthy Texas cattleman, had a grudge against James 'Dog' Kelley, the mayor of Dodge, and decided to kill him. In the early morning hours he rode up to Kelley's two-room cabin and fired his revolver into it, hoping to hit his sleeping victim. He did. His victim, however, was not Kelley but the unfortunate Dora Hand, also known as Fannie Keenan, an actress popular in Dodge. Unknown to Kenedy, Kelley had fallen ill and had been taken away for treatment, leaving the use of his cabin to Dora and another actress. Poor Dora had been sleeping in the mayor's bed and was killed instantly by the

A cowboy band in Dodge City, Kansas in 1886.

buried in the new Prairie Grove Cemetery, north of the town.

'Most places are satisfied with one abode for the dead. In the grave there is no distinction,' the Dodge City *Times* had intoned in September 1877, 'and yet Dodge boasts two burying spots, one for the tainted, whose very souls were steeped by immorality, and who have generally died with their boots on. "Boot Hill' is the somewhat singular title applied to [this] burial place. The other is not designated by any particular title, but is supposed to contain the bodies of those who died with a clean sheet on their bed.'

Bat Masterson was a favorite son of Dodge City. He was there in its formative years as a buffalo hunter. After serving as a police officer in Dodge he was elected in November, 1877 as sheriff of Ford County, of which Dodge City was the county seat, and he brought in a number of badmen to stand trial. Bat was justly celebrated in his own time, unlike his friend and colleague Wyatt Earp, who gained his legendary fame after he died, chiefly through his highly imaginative 'biography' written (and some say mostly invented) by journalist Stuart N Lake and published in 1931. The Leavenworth, Kansas, *Times* of 28 January 1879 described Bat as 'one of the most noted men of the southwest, as cool, brave and daring as anyone who ever drew a pistol.' Billy Dixon, famous frontiersman, likened Bat to 'a chunk of steel' and 'anything that struck him in those days always drew fire.'

Bat's exploits are too numerous to relate here but one in particular should be included because it demonstrates the shifting fortunes of lawmen-gunfighters of the period. In April 1881 Jim Masterson, now ex-marshal, was a partner of A J Peacock in a dance hall and saloon business in Dodge. Jim had an argument with Peacock which resulted in guns being drawn and shots fired, Peacock being backed by his bartender Al Updegraff, but no one was hurt. At that time Bat, no longer a peace officer, was at Tombstone, Arizona, prospecting for gold. Jim telegraphed his brother asking him to return to Dodge and help him in his difficulties.

Bat came on the first train and immediately confronted Peacock and Updegraff in the street. At a distance of 20 feet he called to them: 'I have come over a thousand miles to settle this. I know you are heeled [armed]. Now fight.' All three started firing, then they took cover and continued shooting for about five minutes until their guns were empty. Updegraff was the only one hurt, shot through the lungs (fortunately he recovered). Bat was arrested by police officers and fined 10 dollars and costs for disturbing the peace.

'Great indignation was manifested and is still felt by the citizens against the Masterson party,' thundered the *Ford County Globe*, 'as the shooting was caused by a private quarrel, and the parties who were anxious to fight should

have had at least a thought for the danger they were causing disinterested parties on the street and in business houses . . . the citizens are thoroughly aroused and will not stand any more foolishness. They will not wait for the law to take its course if such an outrage should again occur.'

Nevertheless, the good citizens of Dodge forgave their favorite, if wayward, son and in the Fourth of July celebration of 1885, the genial Bat was elected the 'Most Popular Man in Dodge' and was presented with a gold-headed cane that he carried proudly for many years. With Dodge changing its character from wild young cowtown to mature respectability, Bat said goodbye to the place and drifted to other parts of the West. In 1902 he settled in New

'Wild Bill' Hickok was shot dead by Jack McCall while playing poker in a saloon in Deadwood City, Dakota Territory.

York City and became a successful sports writer on the *Morning Telegraph*. He died at his desk from a heart attack in 1921.

During the cattle boom of the late 1870s and early 1880s more than 250,000 head a year were shipped from Dodge. Not all the herds trailed into Dodge were sent east on the railroad, many were 'through cattle' that were driven on up to the northern ranges of Montana, Wyoming, and the Dakotas. Dodge City's rollicking reign as Queen of the Cowtowns ended in 1885 when the long-threatened quarantine line, under mounting pressure from the farmers, was extended all the way to the western border of the state, and Texas cattle were forbidden to enter Kansas.

A scene on a trail drive from a painting, *Cattle Drive* by Charles M Russell, with a herd stretching to the horizon.

4
COWBOY
LIFE
AND
CHARACTER

I believe I would know an old cowboy
in hell with his hide burnt off. It's
the way they stand and walk and talk.
Teddy Blue, *We Pointed Them North*

64

'During the last fifteen years the American cowboy has occupied a place sufficiently important to entitle him to a considerable share of public attention,' wrote Joseph Nimmo, Jr in *Harper's New Monthly Magazine* of November 1886. Over the last 100 years the attention has never ceased. Probably more books, both pulp and serious, have been published and more movies made about cowboys than any other historical character. Dime novels and the Buffalo Bill Wild West show transformed the rider of the range from equestrian working man to a paladin of the plains, a galloping, six-gun hero, scourge of evil Indians, snarling Mexicans, and white bandits. But when he first made his mark on the American nation the cowboy did not enjoy a good press. He was much misrepresented and misunderstood.

'When a [Western] town is sacked, or a railroad train is robbed by masked men,' William M Thayer commented in his book *Marvels of the New West*, 1888, 'it is heralded throughout the eastern States as the crime of cowboys, when more likely a gang of professionals from New York or Chicago perpetrated the deed. That there are bad cowboys must be admitted; but, as a class, they are not the desperadoes and cut-throats which many eastern papers represent them to be.'

However, as we have seen in the previous chapter, the trail-driving cowboy, particularly the wild Texas variety, brought much of the criticism from the 'civilized' quarters upon his own neck by his crazy antics when he reached trail's end in a cattle town. They were pictured in eastern eyes as pirates of the prairie, armed with a brace of pistols, swaggering or riding through a town, firing their guns all over the place, intent on terrorizing the decent folk. The Texans themselves looked upon their trail's-end activities as harmless, well-earned fun after the long and grueling drive. To the settled townsfolk and farmers of the day, sober and constrained, the transient and ebullient cowboy, 'half horse, half man,' was a necessary evil

A line camp on the Matador Ranch in Texas. A cowboy is giving his partner a haircut outside their dugout shelter.

who brought in cattle, thereby generating profit and wealth (though the ordinary cowhand enjoyed little benefit from the economy he stimulated).

'The typical Texas cowboy,' as described in the *Annals of Kansas*, 1882, 'wears a white hat with a gilt cord and tassel, high top boots, leather pants, a woollen shirt . . . On his heels he wears a pair of jingling Mexican spurs, as large around as a tea-cup. When he feels well (and he always does when full of what he calls "Kansas sheep-dip"), the average cowboy is a bad man to handle. Armed to the teeth, well mounted, and full of his favorite beverage, the cowboys will dash through the principal streets of a town, yelling like Comanches. This they call "Cleaning out the town".'

To far-away city dwellers, the servants of industry grim and gray, who enjoyed dime novel escapism about the Wild West and gazed with admiration at the galloping, whooping, rope-twirling, Stetson-hatted riders of Buffalo Bill's show and similar exhibitions, the cowboy was a romantic figure, a roving cavalier of free spirit who roamed the great Wild West as he pleased. The public at large was not aware of the cowboy's work, his dirty and hardworking life, nor were they interested in such mundane stuff. The paying public wanted plenty of shooting, riding, killing of Indians and badmen, and lots of exciting adventure. The pulp magazines and the Honorable Buffalo Bill Cody did not disappoint them (to be fair to Cody, most of his performers were, or had been, genuine cowboys).

The same was true of Hollywood and the film industry for many years. Hardly a cow was shown on the screen; cowboys, with no apparent work to do, were portrayed as drifters seeking trouble, adventure, wrongs to put right, and badmen to put down. In the last thirty years, some film makers of integrity have presented the working cowboy in his proper context, in particular in *Red River* (1948), *Will Penny* (1967) and *The Culpepper Cattle Company* (1972). The Hollywood presentation of the cow-

Two cowboys preparing to shoe a mustang horse at the Blue River Horse Camp on the Apache Reservation in Arizona, 1909.

boy as a figure of pure entertainment surely reached its most puerile level with the introduction of the sanitized 'singing cowboy' of which the exemplars were Gene Autry and Roy Rogers. A favorite story of mine which captures the song-a-scene spirit of this genre concerns an apocryphal movie in which a cowboy faces his intended posse and with as much anger as he could portray, tells them: 'Those varmints have killed my dear mother, raped my darlin' wife, stole my life's savings, and burned down my ranch! I'm gonna ride out and hunt 'em down. Are you with me, men?'

To which the posse reply: 'Sure, but give us a song before we go.'

Most certainly the old time cowboys used to sing, low and crooning to the cattle to soothe the savage breast in order to prevent a stampede, and round the campfire after the day's work. But their songs did not praise the beauty of the moon over the Rockies. They mostly sang plaintive ditties reflecting the hard, monotonous life they led, about cattle and horses, in much the same spirit as the blacks sang the blues:

> The cowboy's life is a dreary, weary one
> He works all day in the setting of the sun
> And then his day's work is not done
> For there's his night guard to go on
> A cowboy's life is a dreary, dreary life
> Some say it's free from care
> Rounding up the cattle from morn till night
> On the bald prairie so bare

To his range or trail boss the cowboy was more often than not a loyal, industrious, and courageous worker, willing to risk his life (for little pay) many times over on the long trail, especially during the hazards of a river crossing or a stampede. 'I wish I could find words to express the trueness, the bravery, the hardihood, the sense of honor, the loyalty to their trust and to each other,' said Charles Goodnight, the legendary cattleman, of the old trail hands. 'They kept their places around the herd under all circumstances, and if they had to fight they were always ready. Timid men were not among them—the life did not fit them.'

As for himself, the cowboy harbored the notion that he was a superior being, a horseman, a

hired hand worth his salt. His free spirit acknowledged no master and he viewed with contempt those who worked on foot. By the very nature of his arduous labor and wilderness environment, the ordinary cowhand was, as Goodnight bears testimony, mostly a tough hombre who considered himself the equal to, if not better than, any man he might encounter. Some men might have more business savvy, more wealth and power, but out there on the range or the trail, man to man in the game of survival, he was the equal of any. The cowboy's pride in being a free agent would not allow him to voice that he 'worked' for somebody; he would say that he 'rode' for a particular 'brand' or 'ranch.'

Theodore Roosevelt, the first 'cowboy' president of the United States, a man of much vigor and wide intelligence and education, was greatly impressed by the West and the cowboy type, with whom he lived and worked in the early 1880s when he established a ranch in the Dakota Territory. On the question of cowhands being dangerous company, Roosevelt stated in 1884:

'The cowboys are a much misrepresented set of people. It is a popular impression that when one goes among them he must be prepared to shoot . . . I have taken part with them in the round-up, have eaten, slept, hunted, and herded cattle with them, and have never had any difficulty. If you choose to enter rum shops with them or go on drinking sprees with them it is easy to get into difficulty out there as it would be in New York, or anywhere else. But if a man minds his own business and at the same time shows that he is fully prepared to assert his rights—if he is neither a bully nor a coward and keeps out of places in which he has no business to be—he will get along as well as in Fifth Avenue. I have found them a most brave and hospitable set of men . . . there are many places in our cities where I should feel less safe than I would among the wildest cowboys.'

In his cowboy days Teddy Roosevelt mostly kept his mouth shut and his ears and eyes open. He learned the ways of the Westerner, came to admire his tough frontier qualities, and in turn the bespectacled eastern dude, by throwing himself wholeheartedly into the business of being a cowboy, earned the Westerners' respect. Although Roosevelt treated the Wild West with some circumspection, he stood for no nonsense when the chips were down, as the following incident will show.

Out searching for lost horses, Roosevelt came upon a primitive hotel and decided to put up there for the night. As he approached the place, he heard gunshots from the barroom and thought twice about entering. But it was a cold night and there was nowhere else to go. So in he went. The bartender was wearing 'the kind of smile worn by men who are making believe to like what they don't like,' Roosevelt wrote in his autobiography. The cause of the trouble was a shabby individual, loud-mouthed, cursing, who had been shooting at the clock. 'As

A cowboy preparing to rope cattle during a roundup on the Sherman Ranch in Kansas, 1900. Inset: Roy Rogers.

soon as he saw me he hailed me as "Four eyes," in reference to my spectacles, and said, "Four eyes is going to treat." I joined in the laugh and got behind the stove and sat down, thinking to escape notice.'

But the badman was intent on trouble. He followed Roosevelt, leaned over him, a gun in each hand, and abused him with foul words. Roosevelt sized the man up, noticed the way he was standing, with his heels close together in an unstable position, and quickly decided on his next move. When the man again demanded that Roosevelt set up the drinks, 'Four eyes' rose from his chair, saying, 'Well, if I've got to, I've got to'—and swiftly struck the braggart on the chin with his right fist, hit him with his left, and again with his right (Teddy had learned to box at Harvard). The badman fell backwards, firing his guns in the air, and banged his head against the corner of the bar, which rendered him unconscious. Roosevelt removed the fellow's pistols and had no more trouble with him.

In the late 1880s eastern writers changed their attitude toward the cowboy. They transformed him from rogue to romantic character. But the typical working day of a real cowboy was anything but romantic. 'There was no romance in getting up at four in the morning,' wrote Texan Ramon Adams, 'eating dust behind the trail herd, swimming muddy and turbulent rivers, nor in doctoring screw worms [in cattle], pulling stupid cows from bog holes, sweating in the heat of summer, and freezing in the cold of winter.' There were few if any easy jobs in 19th century America for the ordinary working man, and the cowboy's job was harder than most. Long hours and low pay, over the years it ranged from 25 to 40 dollars a month.

If the old time cowboy's courage and physical endurance were great, his intellectual outlook was sharply restricted and his social development limited to adjustment to the rough and

Opposite above: A Wyoming cowboy. Below: C N Dunlap, the foreman at the Watson ranch near Kearney, Buffalo County, Nebraska, photographed in 1888. He is holding horns of a steer.

rigid code of the cattle country. Nothing else concerned him but the cows he herded, the horses he rode, and the taciturn comrades he lived and worked with. A trail drive was an arduous monotonous task, to be sure, but it was something to look forward to, for it took the country cowboy out of his parochial surroundings into new terrain and towns that, save for the opportunity of the trail drive, he might never have seen. Most cowboys could not read or write. But what he lacked in letters and learning he made up for in other abilities developed to suit his environment. He could sense danger swiftly. His reflexes were quick. He was trained in observation and could assess with surprising quickness and accuracy the peculiarities of a bunch of cattle. Most cowboys were born to the saddle and possessed a wonderful affinity with horses.

The cowhand was suspicious of strangers, and judged a man by his ability to measure up to the cowboy's code. In speaking he compressed his thoughts and ideas into the fewest possible words. He had a whimsical turn of humor. A cowboy on being asked if the water

The Monte Deal at Ojo Caliente by Frederic Remington as it appeared in *Harper's New Monthly Magazine* in 1893.

in a particular hole was fit to drink, might answer: 'Yup, it's pretty thick, though, you'll have to chew it a little before you swallow it.' Organized religion played a small part in the cowhand's daily round of living. Indeed, many were open scoffers; a vulgar parody of the Bible was widespread throughout the West. Nevertheless, the average cowboy was raised in a Christian home and taught by Christian parents. Out on the plains he did not attend church regularly, if at all, nor did he read the Bible; yet the cowboy had faith in himself, in his fellow men and, in an ambiguous way, in God. Out of this came the code that demanded an honest, straight-dealing way of life, a practical kind of Christianity succinctly expressed by Jesse Chisholm, the old trader who blazed the Chisholm Trail:

'I don't know nothing about the Bible. I have no use for preachers. But no man ever came to me hungry and went away unfed. All my life I have tried to live at peace with my fellow man and be his brother. The rest I leave with the Great Spirit who placed me here, and who I trust to do all things well.'

The so-called code of the West was a set of unwritten rules tacitly understood and mostly adhered to by all cowboys and plainsmen. Simple rules based on practical, reciprocal altruism. A Westerner freely fed a hungry stranger and gave him shelter because he could find himself in the same needy situation. Likewise he would ask no questions of a stranger. A cattleman would return stray cows to their rightful owner because he would want his own animals returned to him. A cowboy was expected to be loyal to his outfit, even to death, and he seldom failed in this duty. Cattlemen believed in the contractual bond of a man's word; a verbal assurance sealed with a handshake was considered enough in many cases.

A strict rule was to respect women, who were few enough in the West and all the more reason to treat with high regard. Another rigid rule was a swift noose for a horse or cattle thief. According to the code of the West one did not pull a gun on an unarmed man, nor did one shoot a man in the back or from a concealed position (although professional gunmen paid no heed to this stricture of fair play). When two riders met on the trail, passed the time of day and rode on in their different ways, it was a violation of the code for either of them to look over his shoulder at the departing rider, for this would be regarded as an act of distrust, as if expecting a bullet in the back. There were many other minor rules of social etiquette that governed cowboy life. A tenderfoot learned quickly what not to do.

A cowboy's clothes and accoutrements were distinctive, and dashing to eastern eyes, but each item of dress was worn for comfort and convenience; a cowboy's costume was, above all, a practical attire that had evolved over the years to suit and serve him in the terrain and the tasks in which he labored. No other item of his dress symbolizes so singularly the spirit of

When two bulls got into a fight, sometimes the cowboys would bet on the action. An illustration by W A Rogers.

the cattle country than the 'ten gallon' hat, so called for its usefulness in serving as a handy water bucket for horse and man. Its wide brim not only sheltered him from the sun and the rain but in winter the brim could be tied down to protect the ears from frostbite. The high crown gave space to keep the head cool. The hat (most probably made by the J B Stetson Company of Philadelphia) also served as a whip when required to urge on the cowboy's mount or slap a lagging cow into line; it could be used as a flag to send signals over long distances, and at the day's end it fanned the

fitting top protected the leg from cactus, thorny brush, snake bites, chafing against the saddle fender, and it prevented dirt and gravel from getting inside. Cowboys preferred to have their boots custom made and gladly paid highly for a good pair. 'The men of our outfit,' wrote Granville Stuart in *Forty Years on the Frontier*, 1925, 'used to pay 25 dollars a pair for made-to-order riding boots when the best store boots in Helena [Montana] were 10 dollars a pair.' The finest boots came from the workshop of H J Justin, who had set himself up in business in 1879 in the little town of Spanish Fort, Texas, at the

Horse racing was another way of breaking the monotony, as shown in this illustration from *The Graphic*, 1892.

campfire into life and served as the weary cowhand's pillow. The first successful Stetson model, called the 'Boss of the Plains,' retailed in different grades from five to thirty dollars. A cowhand would strive to obtain the best 'J B' he could afford.

Good, close-fitting boots were of great importance to the working cowboy. The distinctive design of the cowboy boot was determined by utility: the narrow pointed toe slipped easily into the stirrup, the high under-slung heel kept the foot firmly anchored in the stirrup, especially when roping an animal. The high, close-

Red River crossing on the Chisholm Trail. Cowboy boots were made strictly for riding and discouraged walking, and that suited the cowhand just fine. When he did walk it was the narrow-footed boots and his bowed legs that gave the cowboy his curious gait.

Spurs were worn all the time. Not only a necessary part of his working equipment, they served as a flashy insignia of his profession. Basically all Western spurs were constructed the same but the types of rowels varied in size and design, from small star shapes to the big Mexican-Texan sunburst type with long prongs. A cowboy seldom used his spurs to hurt or lacerate his horse, but merely to prod and signal his trained pony into quick action. Cowboys often fixed little metal pendants called jinglebobs to their spurs to give a pleasing tinkling sound as they moved.

The tough leather chaps a cowboy wore protected his legs from sharp brush, cactus, rope burns, and from the horns of cattle. Cowboys wore different types of chaps depending on the

a constantly used saddle molded itself to the rider's contours. A cowhand might be foolish enough to gamble away all his other possessions, but never his saddle. The heavy cowboy saddle with its high cantle and fork, the latter surmounted by a horn, derived in shape and utility from the saddle used by the California and Mexican vaqueros, who had developed the Spanish war saddle of the Conquistadores to suit the needs of handling cattle from horseback. The saddle horn was used for taking a turn of the lariat in order to anchor a cow after it had been roped, a technique known as a

geography of the cattle country. Texans wore leather for the reasons stated above. On the cold northern plains riders favored chaps covered with Angora wool, the inside legs being made of soft calfskin; and the wool cover, or wolf, goat, or bear skin was worn with the hair outside. Warm woolly chaps were used extensively in the winter.

The saddle was the cowboy's throne. He would pay a lot for a good one, as it would most likely serve him well for all his working life. For a man riding most of the day, a comfortable saddle was of paramount importance;

A cowboy roping a longhorn in the 1870s. Notice the horse's stance and the method of wrapping the rope.

'dally,' from the Spanish *da la vuelta*, meaning 'give a turn.' The Anglo-American cowboy, who inherited many names and phrases from the vaquero, mangled the words to 'dolly welter,' then 'dally.'

The word 'lariat', as has been mentioned, comes from *la reata* for rope, and 'lasso' from *lazo* for noose. But the cowhand always called a rope a rope and, loosely coiled, hanging from his pommel within easy reach, it was an essential piece of equipment. Apart from roping animals, it could be employed to form a makeshift corral for horses on the trail or range, for pulling cattle and wagons out of the mire, and various other tasks—not forgetting the hanging of horse and cattle thieves. The quirt or short whip, usually secured to the wrist, was a useful aid to a cowboy and is seen in many of Remington's paintings and drawings, yet is rarely seen in Western movies.

The cowboy's bandana, or handkerchief (usually a red one), worn loosely knotted around his neck, served a number of purposes: it shielded his neck from the sun, wiped the sweat from his eyes, it masked his nose and mouth against the swirling, choking trail dust. His vest, or short sleeveless jacket, was most suitable for a mounted working man; it gave a measure of warmth, ease of movement, and provided handy pockets required for various little items. A cowboy's hands were inured to hard work but he wore gloves to protect his hands against thorns, rope burns, and hot branding irons.

When a trail-driving cowboy hit town he dressed himself in his finest eye-catching attire. He was proud of his calling and he wanted to be noticed. A correspondent of the Toledo, Ohio, *Blade* on a visit to the cattle town of Ellsworth, Kansas, in 1872 reported to his readers that, 'I noticed one young fellow fixed out in so many colors, I fancied he must belong to a circus, but was informed he was a TEXAS DROVER. He was certainly gorgeous, and I have no doubt he enjoyed to the fullest extent the attention we gave him. His hat was fancifully braided straw, and around the crown was a string of gaudy bead band . . . His jacket was made to hang open in front, so that his shirt, made of as many colors as Joseph's coat of old, might be allowed to add to the general effect. His trousers had silver lace down the seams, and were tucked in his boots so that they would not hide the boots, which were striped with red morocco, running up and down the legs.'

The cowboy rode with native skill and authority but without finesse, his legs at full stretch, his feet planted firmly in broad, comfortable, leather-clad stirrups; in brush and cactus country the stirrups would be encased in protective leather hoods called 'taps,' from the Spanish *tapaderas*. Generally speaking cowboys were good to their horses, but they were not soft in their treatment. A cowhand worked long and hard and he made damn sure that he got the utmost from his mount. The cowhorse was crossbred from the feral mustang and other domestic bloodlines; the resulting pony possessed an inherent 'cow sense' and was surefooted over rugged terrain.

'Texas [cowboy] ponies are small, tough, and unkempt in appearance,' stated an article on the cattle country in *Harper's New Monthly Magazine* of July 1884. 'Seldom groomed, shod, or stabled, they run loose until wanted for the saddle or the harness, when they are driven in from the range to a pen. Picking up their own living on grass only, they cannot stand the hard work of grain-fed animals; consequently two or three sets must be provided. Each is ridden in turn until exhausted, when another lot takes its place. For this reason at least double the number of horses in daily use must be kept on hand during the season of the round-ups.'

The most prized of ponies in the cattle country was a good 'cutting horse,' one trained to cut out, or separate a particular cow from the herd, a technique that required skilled riders and skilled mounts. 'A [cutting] horse that knows what is wanted goes quietly through the herd while you are looking for your brand,' wrote Reginald Aldridge, a Montana cattleman in 1884, 'then, when you have singled out the animal and urged her on gently to the edge of the herd, [the horse] perceives at once which is the one to be ejected. When you have got the cow close to the edge, you make a little rush behind her, and she runs out; but likely as not as soon as she finds herself outside the herd she tries to get back again, and makes a sudden wheel to the left past you. Instantly your horse turns to the left, and runs along between her and the herd so that she cannot get in. Then she tries to dodge in behind you. The moment she turns, your horse stops and wheels round again, always keeping between the cow and the herd, till she gives it up and runs out to be cut where you want her. A good cutting horse will do all this with the reins lying loose upon his neck.'

Every cattle ranch had its roughstring of horses, unbroken broncs, young range horses, and untamed buckers. The words 'bucker' and 'bucking' originated in the Northwest where a cowboy was known as a 'buckeroo,' the Americanized version of vaquero. Breaking horses to the saddle was a specialized job, known mostly

Left: A Montana cowboy and his pack horse, together with all of the equipment needed on the trail. Top right: A cowboy spur with a large rowel. Right: A Justin cowboy boot that was manufactured in 1900.

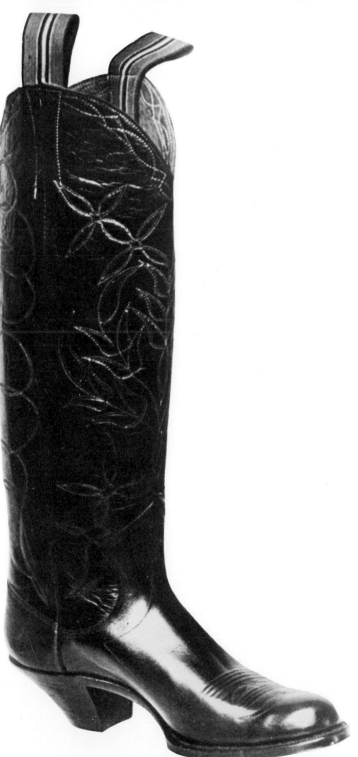

as 'busting' or 'twisting.' A bronco-buster was usually a professional horse tamer. First he would rope the horse in a corral, tie the rope to a 'snubbing' post, then swing his heavy saddle on the animal's rearing back, then mount and ride the bucking, twisting bronc until he mastered it, applying his quirt every time the horse bucked to unseat him. Unlike the modern rodeo rider who is required to stay in the saddle for eight seconds, the old-time bronco-buster rode the hurricane until it blew itself out.

North American cowboys were not all the Anglo-Saxon type. There were a great many Mexican and Black cowhands. William Loren Katz, in *The Black West*, 1971, tells us that, 'Among the cowboys of the last frontier, five thousand black men helped drive cattle up the Chisholm Trail after the Civil War.' In a typical

The famous Bill Pickett. This man was the black cowboy credited with originating the rodeo sport of bulldogging.

Nat Love, the celebrated black cowboy who was nicknamed 'Deadwood Dick.' This photograph was taken in the 1870s.

trail crew of eight men, at least two were Blacks. With the end of the Civil War, young Blacks headed West in search of a new freedom, a new way of life. Many became cowboys, others favored a homestead and worked the land. Some joined the two regiments of the US Cavalry—the Ninth and the Tenth—all Black except for the officers. The black troopers fought the Indians in a number of campaigns and came to be called the 'Buffalo Soldiers.' The black cavalry rode to the rescue of besieged white soldiers on several occasions.

Some black cowboys turned outlaws, others became famous for their skills and fine characters. Britton Johnson won the reputation of being the best shot on the Texas frontier just after the Civil War. Bose Ikard was a top cowhand held in high regard by his boss, Charles

Isom Dart, one of the more notable of the black cowboys. Later in life, he turned from tending cattle to rustling.

Kansas cowboy Jim Kellerman, photographed in the 1880s. He wears leather chaps, gauntlets and a quirt on the wrist.

Goodnight, who said of him: 'There was a dignity, a cleanliness, and reliability about him that was wonderful . . . His behavior was very good in a fight . . . I have trusted him farther than any living man. He was my detective, banker, and everything else in Colorado, New Mexico, and any other wild country I was in. The nearest and only bank was at Denver, and when we carried money I gave it to Bose, for a thief would never think of robbing him—never think of looking in a Negro's bed for money.'

Nat Love was a famous black cowboy who won the nickname 'Deadwood Dick.' Born a slave in Tennessee in 1854, at the age of 15, he was a free man, and headed West to become a cowboy at 30 dollars a month. He took part in the long drives that trailed the Texas Longhorns to Kansas and other northern cattle towns. Although white cowboys accepted Blacks as able working partners they did not share the bunkhouse or social life in town.

In his autobiography published in 1907, Love relates how he came by his nickname. In the spring of 1876 he helped drive a herd from Arizona to Deadwood City, Dakota Territory. He arrived there in time for the Independence Day celebrations. Nat entered several cowboy competitions, winning a roping contest and a shooting match, and so impressed the spectators that, 'Right there,' in Nat's words, 'the assembled crowd named me "Deadwood Dick" and proclaimed me champion roper of the Western cattle country.' After many years Nat Love left the range to become a railroad Pullman porter.

Isom Dart was, in some respects, the black counterpart of cowboy outlaw Butch Cassidy. Both were affable, laughing, likeable characters who turned from herding cattle to stealing them. Born in slavery in Arkansas in 1849, Dart drifted into south Texas and Mexico, working as a cowhand. With a Mexican partner he started stealing cattle south of the border and selling them in Texas. After a while he turned to prospecting, then earned a living broncobusting. A cattleman said of him that, 'no man understood horses better.'

Another praised him thus: 'I've seen all the

In the dust and heat of the trail drive the cowboys would become filthy. Here some cowboys are bathing in a waterhole.

great riders, but Isom Dart was unexcelled, he could outride any of them.'

Despite his respectable success as bronco-buster, he returned to rustling cattle. He was arrested several times but never jailed. Once, when being taken in by the deputy sheriff of Sweetwater County, Wyoming, the buckboard overturned, leaving the deputy injured and Dart unharmed. Instead of seizing the chance to escape, Dart righted the buckboard and drove the deputy to a doctor in Rock Springs. Then the black outlaw turned himself over to the local law officer. His behavior was so unusual for a suspected rustler that he was judged innocent and released. Isom Dart was shot dead in 1900 by a concealed rifleman, believed to be Tom Horn, the implacable manhunter hired by rich cattlemen to clear the range of rustlers.

Bill Pickett was a celebrated black cowboy who worked on the 110,000-acre 101 Ranch in Oklahoma, owned by the Miller brothers. Zack Miller described Pickett as 'the greatest sweat and dirt cowhand that ever lived.' Born of a Choctaw Indian mother and a black father in 1861, Pickett worked as a cowboy in South America and Texas before signing up with the Miller outfit. The 101 Ranch boasted a number of top hands highly skilled in particular aspects of cowboy expertise. Johnny Brewer was a crack bronco-buster, Jim Hopkins was a master with the rope, and Kurt Reynolds was a splendid all-around cowhand. Bill Pickett specialized in—indeed, invented—the tough cowboy sport of 'bulldogging.'

This involved leaping from the saddle of a moving horse and grabbing a running steer by the horns. Then, with boot heels digging in the dirt to brake the animal, Pickett wrestled the heavy steer into the dirt by twisting its head back and its nose up. He could perform this feat of strength and skill with relative 'ease. And he concluded the act with a spectacular and unique flourish: he would sieze the steer's tender upper lip with his own strong teeth, then flip the animal over by falling to one side and holding on with his bulldog grip until the beast was completely subdued, all the while holding his hands clear to demonstrate that he was gripping the steer with his teeth alone. Bulldogging, or steer wrestling, is today a standard rodeo event but the contestants do not use their teeth in the Pickett manner.

With all this cowboy talent in their outfit, the Millers, in 1905, formed the 101 Ranch Wild West show and opened that year at Madison Square Garden, New York. Bill Pickett and his bulldogging act was a featured attraction. He was billed as 'The Wonderful Negro Pickett. Throwing a Wild Steer by the nose with his Teeth.' He was later billed as the 'Dusky Demon.' The show was a great and continuing success. One day in 1908 in Mexico City, Pickett risked his life in El Toreo, the new bull ring, in one of the strangest contests in cowboy history. The Mexicans viewed Pickett's performance as vulgar and distasteful, lacking the dignity, grace and skill of a bull-fighting torero.

Zack Miller responded to this criticism by offering 1,000 pesos for Mexican charity if any bull fighter in the city could emulate Pickett's performance. None would accept the challenge. The Mexicans countered with another wager: they would pay 5,000 dollars if Pickett would take on a fighting bull. He would not be required to bring down the beast in his inimitable manner, but he must stay in the arena for 15 minutes and maintain close physical contact with the bull for five consecutive seconds. Pickett, then 47 years old, accepted the highly dangerous challenge. Twenty-five thousand excited Mexicans packed El Toreo to witness the black cowboy 'sacrifice himself on the altar of American egotism,' as predicted by the newspaper *El Heraldo*. The event was deemed important enough for President Porfirio Diaz to attend.

The Mexicans had selected a bull noted for its toughness and fighting spirit. The crowd roared with approval as the bull snorted into the arena, 'Viva el toro!' And when Bill Pickett trotted forward on his horse Spradley, the hostile crowd screamed for his death, 'Muerte al Negro de Oklahoma!' As the bull charged, Spradley wheeled and side-stepped to avoid the slashing horns and Pickett could not get close enough to engage the beast. Eventually the bull hooked Spradley's hind quarters, and with his horse screaming in pain, Pickett left the saddle and grabbed the bloody horns. The bull ran on, with Bill digging his heels into the sand trying to slow him. The powerful beast threw the desperate cowboy against the arena wall and attempted to gore him.

Bill staggered to his feet and locked his arms around the bull's neck and, bringing up his knees, squeezed them against the bull's nostrils in an effort to choke off the animal's breath. The heroic Pickett managed to hold on to the monster for the required five seconds, much to the chagrin of the crowd. Bill, suffering three broken ribs and cuts, was carried to safety by his comrades who roped the bull to the ground. Six years later this remarkable man performed before the King and Queen of England. Bill Pickett eventually purchased a 160-acre ranch in Oklahoma and it was there in 1932, aged 71, that he met his death, kicked in the head by a horse he was roping. Zack Miller inscribed the headstone of his grave with the epitaph:

He left a blank that's hard to fill
For there'll never be another Bill.

We opened this chapter with a quotation from Joseph Nimmo, Jr., and we end it with another from him which is apposite to the cow-boy's changing character. 'The cow-boy of to-day [1886], especially on the northern ranges, is an entirely different type from the original cow-boy of Texas. New conditions have produced the change . . . Organization, discipline, and order characterize the new undertakings on the northern ranges . . . the cattle business of that section is now and has from the beginning been carried out upon strictly business principles . . . and a new class of cow-boys has been intro-duced and developed . . . Throughout the north-ern ranges sobriety [and] self-restraint [are] enjoined upon the cow-boys. A great improve-ment is also observable in the cow-boys of Texas. Deeds of violence among them are few.'

Bulldogging, or steer wrestling, is a standard event in a rodeo. Here we see cowboy Tom Ferguson in action in a 1980 rodeo in Salt Lake City, Utah.

The cowboy's quarter hose was a multi-talented animal. Here is one cutting out a calf (painting by Randy Steffen).

5
CATTLE
KINGS

"The New West is the kingdom of cattle
kings. They live royally in this empire
of prairie and valley."
W M Thayer, **Marvels of the New West**

Few working cowboys made a fortune out of the cattle business. Most of them lived out their humble existence with little money in their pockets, spending their hard-earned pay in the same carefree manner in which they faced life. The ordinary cowhand harbored simple ambitions and requirements and lacked the aspiration, the business acumen and the education to make it big in the cattle industry. Some remarkable characters, however, made the transition from common cowboy to cattle king. Charles Goodnight was a magnificent example.

Born in Illinois in 1836, he moved to Texas with his family when he was ten. Brought up in the Brazos River country deep in the Texas plains, young Charlie became a capable cowhand, a skilled bronco-buster, and early developed an ambition to be a cattle owner. In 1856 he and his stepbrother took on the responsibility for caring for some 500 cows of the neighboring CV Ranch. Instead of cash payment the boys were allowed to keep as their own every fourth calf that was born to the herd, and in four years they possessed 180 head. Then came the Civil War, and in service with the Confederacy, Charlie served with distinction in the Texas Rangers and engaged in many fights against the Indians, who, taking advantage of the war, raided settlements bereft of men.

On leaving the Rangers early in 1864, Goodnight set about rounding up his cattle, which during his absence had grown to 5,000 head; this number he boosted by purchasing more and putting his brand on mavericks and by the spring of 1865 the Goodnight herd totaled 8,000 head. An innovator as well as being a hard-headed businessman, Goodnight decided against the general trend of cattle drovers who planned to drive their Longhorns to the railhead at Sedalia, Missouri for shipment east. He set his sights on blazing a new trail, west through Texas, then north into New Mexico and even Colorado, with the idea of selling his beef to the military posts, Indian reservations, and mining towns. The trek would entail passing through Indian country and, even more formidable crossing a waterless stretch of the Staked Plains for the best part of 100 miles, from the Middle Concho to the Horsehead crossing on the Pecos River.

While considering this hazardous journey,

Goodnight met up with Oliver Loving who was generally regarded as the best trail driver in Texas. Loving was prepared to try the route and they joined partnership, merging their herds. In June 1866 they set out with 2,000 head and 18 riders to establish the celebrated Goodnight-Loving Trail. They were accompanied by the first chuckwagon, another idea originated by Goodnight; he adapted an army wagon for the purpose, fitting it with an upright chuck or kitchen box at the rear. The chuck box contained compartments to hold provisions and utensils and its tailgate door dropped down to form a table on which the cook could work. The chuckwagon carried a water barrel, wood for the fire, the crew's bedrolls and other equipment. The idea was taken up by other drovers and the chuckwagon became a necessary vehicle on the long drives.

The march across the Staked Plains was a bitter test for the tough Longhorns and the hardy cowboys. By the time they reached the Pecos they were in a pitiable, parched condition. 'When the cattle reached the water they had no sense at all,' Goodnight recalled. 'They stampeded into the stream, swam right across it, then doubled back before they stopped to drink.' About 100 head were killed in the mad rush for water, making a total loss of 300 for the entire drive to Fort Sumner, New Mexico, where government agents paid eight cents a pound for all the steers to feed the reservation Indians. Here, Goodnight and Loving parted company, the latter driving the cows and calves on to Denver, Colorado.

Goodnight returned to Texas with 12,000 dollars in gold packed on a mule's back, intent on buying and driving another profitable herd up the new trail to New Mexico. He nearly lost the gold when the mule bolted one night, but Charlie managed to recover the four-legged fortune.

Opposite top, left to right: Charles Goodnight—the cowboy who became a cattle king—co-founder of the Goodnight-Loving trail; Joseph G McCoy, the pioneer cattleman who opened the beef market at Abilene, Kansas; Granville Stuart, a pioneer cattleman of Montana; Richard King, the founder of the King Ranch in Texas; John Chisum, the New Mexico cattle king. Bottom: An etching of a whole gallery of early cattle barons. Although they are well dressed in the pictures, they all started as cowboys.

Jared L. Brush.

Charles Lux.

R. G. Head.

John H. Iliff.

Thos. H. Lawrence.

John W. Snyder.

John T. Lytle.

The Goodnight-Loving partnership ended in 1867 when Loving died from a wound he received during an attack by Comanches. Charlie survived the Indian perils of the Goodnight-Loving Trail and prospered. But he had his financial setbacks. In 1869 he established a cattle ranch in Colorado and was set as a cattle king when the Panic of 1873, caused by falling beef prices and the closing of several banks, wiped his fortune away.

Most men would have been crushed by such a reverse. But not Charles Goodnight. He had an indomitable spirit. He could handle any problem, like the time he told Dick Wootten 'to go to hell!' Wootten, an old mountain man, had built a road across Raton Pass in southern Colorado and, with rifle in hand, demanded a toll of ten cents a head for cattle to use the pass. Oliver Loving paid it grudgingly but when Goodnight reached the pass he told Wootten where to go, turned his herd east and blazed a new route across Trincheras Pass, cutting 100 miles off the distance to Pueblo. After losing his fortune, Goodnight returned to Texas to make another one. He drove a herd of 1500 cattle across 300 miles of wilderness in 1876 and established a ranch in the Palo Duro Canyon in the Texas Panhandle.

The following year he entered into partnership with John Adair, a wealthy Irishman, and with Adair's investment of 500,000 dollars developed the enormous JA Ranch in Palo Duro Canyon into a kingdom of one million acres and 100,000 cattle. Goodnight managed this by employing ruthless business methods; buying some public land and simply appropriating the rest (a standard practice among cattle kings) by occupation. In five years Adair's investment had returned a clear profit of 512,000 dollars. By cross breeding the native Longhorn with imported Shorthorn and Hereford cattle, Goodnight developed one of the finest beef herds in the nation.

Charlie's cowboys either loved him or disliked him, but they all respected him and worked hard to gain his approval. Even in old age he presented an impressive figure. 'He was massive of frame, quick of move-

The railroad carried western cattle to the eastern markets. This is one of the early air-polluting steam engines.

Opposite top: A Union Pacific locomotive at Wyoming Station, near the Little Laramie River in 1868. Bottom: The Cheyenne Club, a gathering place for Wyoming ranchers. Inset: A track-laying crew on the Union Pacific Railroad.

ment, and powerful of physique,' wrote J Evetts Haley, Goodnight's biographer. 'His tremendous head, set forward on his broad shoulders, was crowned with a great shock of hair. From beneath shaggy brows his eyes flashed and burned into every man he faced.' Like all cowboys, he was bowlegged and awkward on his feet, but in the saddle his bearing was natural and easy, he became part of the horse. Goodnight had a hatred of hypocrites, liars, and rustlers. He admired a man with spirit. There is a story about a cowhand who approached him for a job. Charlie riveted the man with his fierce eyes and said bluntly: 'I hear you are a cow thief.'

The man returned the hard gaze and replied: 'I hear you stole a few in the early days.' Goodnight hired him and was not disappointed.

Ever the innovator, Charlie produced a new species of animal—the cattalo—by crossing Polled Angus with the buffalo. He designed an improved, safer sidesaddle for women riders and the Goodnight sidesaddle was widely used in the West. On a simple diet of mostly meat and black coffee, and a box of cigars a day, Charles Goodnight lived to a grand old age, dying in 1929 at 93. The town of Goodnight in the Texas Panhandle was named after him.

John Simpson Chisum, an associate of Goodnight, also started his trail to the top as a cowhand in Texas. He eventually became one of the biggest individual cattle owners in North America, with between 60,000 and 100,000 head ranging over a vast tract of New Mexico. He was called 'King of the Pecos,' from the river of that name which watered his domain. Born in Tennessee in 1824 he spent his early years on the family farm and such was his childhood interest and knowledge of cattle that he was dubbed 'Cow John.' He came to know cattle so thoroughly that Goodnight said of him: 'He could count three grades of cattle at once and count them even if they were going at a trot.' On one occasion when Chisum was driving a herd into New Mexico, a drover named Adams was following with another herd. The Adams herd was plagued with stampedes, so Chisum

rode back to see if he could help. He cast his expert eye over the Longhorns and settled on a large, one-eyed steer. 'Cut that one out,' he advised Adams, 'take him down to the river and kill him.' Adams did just that and the series of stampedes ended.

John was 13 when the family moved to Lamar County in east Texas. He had little schooling but learned to read and write and developed a good business sense. Striking out on his own, he bought a small herd of Longhorns and trailed them eastward to Shreveport in Louisiana, one of the first drives out of Texas. But he made no money on the endeavor and tried again, to Little Rock in Arkansas, and made a small profit. He tried other business deals in real estate, and as a building contractor, and was later elected county clerk of Lamar County. After the Civil War he entered the packing business. His function in the firm of Clark, Chisum & Wilber was to buy cattle in Texas and drive them to the packing plant at Fort Smith, Arkansas.

The business, however, went bankrupt and Chisum made an agreement with Charles Goodnight to trail herds across the Pecos and hand them over to Goodnight, who would drive them up to Colorado to supply beef to the mining camps and to stock the new ranches. With the ill-starred packing venture behind him, Chisum trailed thousands of Longhorns out of Texas over the next few years. But he was not completely finished with the packing episode. Documents signed by Chisum and other executives of the company had been given for cattle purchased for the plant, promissory notes to the amount of 90,000 dollars. Chisum had managed to ease himself out of the ensuing legal action, and made his deal with Goodnight.

In 1867 Chisum moved his holdings to New Mexico and built his ranch headquarters at the Bosque Grande on the Pecos, some thirty miles north of present-day Roswell. Here, Chisum's kingdom of open range, his by 'right' of occupation and use, grew and grew until it covered a fifth of the entire New Mexico Territory and by 1875 his distinctive brand marked the hides of an estimated 80,000 cattle. Chisum himself did not know the exact number of cattle that he owned. He always reckoned that if a buyer wanted 40,000 head in a hurry, he could fill the order without problems. His brand was the

BUFFALO BILL'S WILD WEST & ROUGH RIDERS

COW BOY FUN. THE

Left: Roy Rogers, one of the most famous of all of the motion picture singing cowboys. This picture of him appeared on the cover of a boys' book in the 1950s. Above: A poster showing some of the thrills and chills that might be enjoyed if one were to attend Buffalo Bill's Wild West Show. Right: William F Cody as seen on an old poster.

HON. W. F. CODY "BUFFALO BILL"

Loading Texas Longhorns in Kansas in the 1870s.

Abilene—the first of the railhead cattle towns.

Long Rail, a straight line extending from shoulder to flank; his cattle were also distinguished with the 'jinglebob' ear cut, in which the ear was split lengthwise so that the lower half dangled, like the jinglebob pendant attached to cowboy spurs.

In 1876 Chisum moved his headquarters from Bosque Grande to South Spring River where he built himself a splendid ranch house fit for a cattle king. With him were his brothers Pitzer and James and their families; John never married and his niece Sally, daughter of James, ran the house in grand style. Chisum's warm and open hospitality, to the humble as well as the important, was known far and wide. Like his peer, Charles Goodnight, Chisum never lost the common touch. Dressed in old comfortable clothes he could often be found working at some job on the ranch. Once, when a stranger approached him while he was working at a menial task, and asked, 'You work for John Chisum?'

The jinglebob king replied, 'Sure do.' When the man asked further how Chisum treated him, John answered, 'He lets me wear his old clothes.'

In common with all owners of vast herds, Chisum was always troubled with rustlers. On one occasion Mexicans ran off 1200 of his horses and Chisum, who rarely carried a gun, took three cowboys and pursued the raiders. He caught up with them and killed three; the rest bolted for their lives. Chisum returned with all the horses. If John could not be out-run or out-gunned, he could be outsmarted. And this is where the old packing plant affair makes a return. There are various versions of the story

but this is the most likely one.

In 1875 an ambitious young lawyer named Tom Catron of Las Vegas, New Mexico had Chisum arrested on fraud charges concerning the unpaid notes tended in obtaining Texas cattle for the dressing plant. Chisum again slipped out of the legal noose. But Catron was determined to make him pay. In league with Jesse Evans, a Kansas drover, and Robert Hunter, head of a Kansas City cattle commission company, Catron formed a plan. Hunter went to Texas and quietly purchased as many of Chisum's promissory notes as he could for ten cents on the dollar. He then rode to South Spring with Evans and fifty cowboys, the latter being gunfighters specially picked for the job. Chisum agreed to sell Hunter 20,000 cattle.

While the cowboy gunmen trailed the great herd to Kansas, Chisum rode with Hunter to Las Vegas to collect payment. Hunter took him to Catron's office and in the presence of the lawyer and other witnesses, threw down a wad of Chisum's promissory notes and obligations to Texas cattlemen, saying, 'There, Chisum, is your settlement.' Apart from calling Hunter a cheat and thief there was little else that the jinglebob king could do. He might have considered leading a bunch of his cowboys after the Kansas drover to bring back his cattle, but he knew there would be a ferocious battle with the gunfighters and many of his boys would surely die. He decided he could live with the loss, and make it up; he certainly could, his cattle continued to increase to an estimated peak of 100,000 head. Later, he attempted to take the sting out of the 'legal rustle' story by saying that he agreed to Hunter's paper deal in order

Ration Day at the Sioux Reservation in Pine Ridge.　　**The Crow Indian Reservation, Montana.**

to settle the whole sorry affair.

It is a matter of argument just how much John Chisum became involved in the Lincoln County War of 1878-79 in which he supported cattleman J H Tunstall against the Murphy-Dolan faction. Tunstall's gunfighter-cowhands included Billy the Kid and it is alleged that Chisum paid the Kid 500 dollars for his services in the Lincoln County conflict. If Chisum was instrumental in turning Billy into an outlaw killer, he also engineered his destruction; he used his considerable influence in getting Pat Garrett elected sheriff of Lincoln County in 1880, and it was Garrett who doggedly hunted down and killed the young outlaw. John Simpson Chisum died in 1884, leaving an estate of some 500,000 dollars.

Of the estimated 10 million Longhorns trailed up from Texas between 1867 to 1890 a large number went to stock the greatest of all open ranges, that of Wyoming, Montana, and the Dakotas. John Wesley Iliff was the first of the cattle kings on the northern plains. Born in Ohio in 1831, son of a wealthy farmer, on completion of his college education he was offered 7,500 dollars by his father to buy a farm, near his own. But John declined the offer, saying, 'Give me the 500 dollars and let me go West.' His father agreed and John went first to Kansas, then to Colorado, where he engaged in the provision business before turning his attention to cattle. Having purchased a small herd from Oliver Loving in Denver, Iliff drove the cattle to the northern part of the Territory for pasturage. The 'college cowboy' knew exactly what he was about.

The Union Pacific Railroad was being pushed

westward through southern Wyoming and the construction gangs set up camp near Cheyenne. Iliff contracted to supply beef to the workers and the soldiers who came to guard them against Indian attacks. By the end of 1868 the railroad was built as far as Cheyenne and Iliff was now able to sell even more beef to the eastern cities. His cattle grew in number and flourished. Like Goodnight, he upgraded his stock by crossing the Longhorns with imported Durham and Hereford bulls, producing fine cattle which provided more meat and milk than the wiry Longhorns. At the time of his death in 1878 he controlled a vast region of pasturage reaching from the South Platte River to Wyoming, and from near the eastern base of the Rockies to Nebraska, over which his 50,000 cattle roamed and grazed.

John Iliff was a cattle king who believed in personally supervising his range domain. He often said that to be successful in the beef business a man had to live with his cows. One of his boasts was that he could ride his range for a week and sleep in a different headquarters cabin every night. He never bothered to carry a gun. His word was the law in the land and his loyal and zealous cowboys enforced it. When Iliff died the Snyder brothers of Texas—cattle kings in their own right—were under contract to deliver 25,000 cattle to his ranch in Weld County, Colorado. Mrs Iliff, familiar with the enterprise and integrity of the brothers, asked them to take charge of the immense herd which her husband left. The Snyder Company assumed that responsibility and the first year shipped 14,000 beeves for her to market. In the spring of 1881 the Snyders purchased the great

the last drop from his STETSON

Above left: A 1972 advertisement for Justin Boots. Above right: A 1920 advertisement for Stetson Hats. Left: *Arizona Cowboy*, **a painting by Frederic Remington. Opposite: Western mining camps offered a ready market for the beef from Texas. Inset:** *Waiting for a Chinook,* **or** *The Last of the 5000,* **painted by Charles Russell in 1887.**

Iliff herd and Mrs Iliff retained an interest in the business.

In the summer of 1880 a stern and scholarly man established a ranch in the richly grassed wilderness of the Judith Basin in central Montana. He was Granville Stuart, 45 years old, and he was destined to impose his iron-willed personality upon the Montana cattle country in no uncertain manner. In his book *Forty Years on the Frontier*, Stuart describes the uninhabited country as he first found it: 'One could travel for miles without seeing so much as a trapper's bivouac. Thousands of buffalo darkened the rolling plains. There was deer, antelope, elk, wolves and coyotes on every hill, and in every ravine and thicket.' Three years later not one buffalo remained on the range.

ture; he was also a capable poker player and a marksman. Prior to setting up his cattle ranch in central Montana, Granville wrote a history of the region, *Montana As It Is*, published in 1865. He helped found the Historical Society of Montana and served as its first secretary.

Following the death of his brother, Granville went into the cattle business. Financed by two bankers named Davis and Hauser, he established the DHS Ranch in the Judith Basin. By October 1880 Stuart had 5,000 cattle feeding off the rich and abundant grass; three years later the herds had proliferated to 12,000 head. DHS cowhand E C 'Teddy Blue' Abbott tells us in his book *We Pointed Them North* how Stuart reacted when over a thousand Blackfeet moved from their reservation across the Missouri, camped near his ranch, and started running off horses and cattle. Stuart, at the head of some of his men, rode into the Indian camp and bluntly told the chiefs to 'pack your tipis and stay across the Missouri—or I will wipe you out!' The Indians knew a resolute man when they saw one, and they crossed the river.

Under Stuart's management the DHS outfit flourished. He brought in thoroughbred Shorthorns to upgrade his stock. He rode with his cowboys and rancher neighbors in the roundups and drove cattle for shipment. In the evenings he wrote about his life on the frontier. Indians were not the only trouble on the Montana range; white rustlers preyed on the growing herds. To combat this, and other problems, Stuart and his fellow ranchers formed the Eastern Montana Stockgrowers Association in 1884. When some members proposed that a small army of cowboys be organized to seek out the rustlers in their concealed cabins and wage open warfare against them, Stuart warned them of the consequences of the law; a man of high morals, he had a profound respect for law and order.

However, when rustlers stole a number of his cattle and horses a few weeks later, Stuart decided to take the law into his own hands. He called a secret meeting of 14 trusted stockmen and advocated swift punishment for the thieves.

'In 1880,' Stuart continues, 'no one heard tell of a cowboy . . . but in the fall of 1883 there were 600,000 cattle on the range [and] the cowboy, with leather chaps, wide hats, gay handkerchiefs, clanking silver spurs . . . had become an institution.'

Born in Iowa in 1835, Stuart was an experienced frontiersman. Having prospected for gold in California and traded with the Indians, he and his brother established a road ranch at a crossing on the Green River, Utah Territory, where they acquired livestock that had become a burden to pioneer wagon trains. Both brothers followed the frontier custom and took Indian wives. When gold strikes were made in Montana in 1863, the Stuart brothers set up a butcher's shop in Bannack and supplied fresh meat to the miners. An industrious pair, they also opened a blacksmith's shop and a dry-goods store in Virginia City. They made a good living but not a fortune. Granville was a self-taught scholar with an abiding love of litera-

Known rustlers, and those caught in the very act, were promptly lynched and left swinging with a notice attached that read 'Horse Thief,' or 'Cattle Thief.' The illegal executioners became known as 'Stuart's Stranglers' and they carried out their grisly self-imposed duty with great effect. The *Mineral Argus* told its readers that, 'Eastern Montana is rapidly reducing the number of horse thieves.'

On a July morning in 1884 Stuart, leading a party of vigilantes, arrived at a place called Bates Point and surrounded a cabin which contained a party of suspected outlaws. Stuart demanded that they come out and surrender. They refused, and opened fire. The vigilantes shot back. Some of the rustlers managed to escape but the others fought on until the cabin was set on fire and, Stuart wrote, 'they were all killed or burned up.' The five who got away were later arrested by the army and given over to a deputy US marshal. The lawman was intercepted by a party of cowboys who took the prisoners and hanged them on a makeshift gallows.

By the autumn of 1884 the Montana ranges had been swept clean of horse and cattle thieves. It is not certain how many men were lynched, some say 75, and many others of dubious character fled the country to escape the 'Stranglers.' Not everyone condoned Stuart's brand of frontier justice. 'There was a lot of bitterness against Granville Stuart after the raids,' recalled Teddy Blue Abbott, 'but he never denied anything, nor did he tell who was with him.' When a woman accused Stuart of hanging 30 innocent men, he accepted full responsibility: 'Yes, madam, and by God, I done it alone.'

The DHS herds continued to grow, and by 1886 numbered 23,000 head. Then came the terrible winter of 1886-87, known as the Great Die-Up in which thousands of cattle perished in the blizzards that swept the now over-stocked ranges. Montana in particular suffered dreadfully. 'In the fall of 1886,' Stuart wrote, 'there were more than one million head of cattle on the Montana ranges and the losses in the "big storm" amounted to twenty million dollars. This was the death knell to the [open] range cattle business on anything like the scale it had been run before.' Stuart lost two-thirds of his stock. The disaster destroyed his interest in the cattle business and he gave it up, turning his attention to politics.

In the years before that cruel and chastening winter the great success of the indigenous cattle kings caught the interest of investors in the eastern States, an interest stimulated to a large extent by a book published in 1881, *The Beef Bonanza; or How to Get Rich on the Plains*, written by General James S Brisbin, who presented somewhat fanciful figures to show that 250,000 dollars invested in cattle would return 810,000 dollars in five years. Promise of such profit could not be ignored. 'The West! The mighty West!' exclaimed Brisbin's propagative prose, 'Where the poor, professional young man, flying from the overcrowded East and the tyranny of a moneyed aristocracy, finds honor and wealth!' A few years later another book,

Below: *A Quarrel Over Cards,* a sketch from a New Mexico ranch by Frederic Remington.
Bottom: Captain King hired Mexican vaqueros to tend the cattle on his vast ranch.

Cattle Raising on the Plains of North America, written by German immigrant Baron von Richthofen, further stimulated investors to put their surplus money into the booming cow business.

News of the beef bonanza reached Europe and triggered a stampede of investors eager to grab an easy and certain profit. From Scotland came the capital to set up the Prairie Land & Cattle Company, which developed into a gigantic enterprise; British money also backed the Wyoming Cattle Ranche Company (the 'e' in Ranche usually indicated that the outfit was British owned) and the Swan Land & Cattle Company. Indeed, of 20 great cattle companies in Wyoming in 1884, half were British financed. But these huge operations were not run by a Goodnight or a Chisum, men with cattle raising in their blood, cowboy patriarchs who rode the range with their men and understood the vagaries of the weather and kept a close eye on every detail.

John Iliff maintained that for a man to be successful in the cattle business he needed to live with his cows. The new ranches were controlled by committees from afar, gentlemen who did not 'wish to know every time one of our cattle falls sick.' Consequently, many of the company outfits suffered from range mismanagement, adverse weather conditions, and falling beef prices. The XIT Ranch, for example, established in 1885, covered three million acres of the Texas Panhandle and boasted 150,000 cattle, yet despite its enormous size never returned a penny in dividends.

Perhaps the most unusual entrepreneur to enter the cattle business in a personal capacity was the Marquis de Mores, a young French nobleman who, in 1881, established in the Dakota Territory a ranch, a meat dressing plant, and a town. De Mores was fired by the dream of making millions of dollars by beef production in order to restore grandeur to the House of Vallombrosa (his family name) and to support the royalist cause in France. Six feet tall, with a moustache waxed to points, and elegant in his manners, de Mores may have looked a fop to the rough Westerners, but he was a dangerous man to challenge. He had a fierce pride and courage and was expert with both sword and pistol. He seemed to possess the necessary assets, both physical and financial, to become a

cattle king. But things did not work out that way.

Born in 1858 to the Duke de Vallombrosa in Paris, he entered the military school of St–Cyr in 1877 and resigned from the army in 1881, having won a reputation as a horseman and duelist. With the family fortune at low ebb, de Mores married American heiress Medora von Hoffman in 1882 and moved to New York, where his millionaire father-in-law gave him a 500,000 dollar dowry and a job in Wall Street. The job did not appeal to the energetic marquis. He wanted to make a spectacular fortune, more millions than his father-in-law possessed, and he saw his opportunity in the much publicized beef bonanza. Partly financed by his father-in-law, de Mores bought 9,000 acres of unsurveyed land in North Dakota for 32,000 dollars; the land, purchased from the Northern Pacific Railroad, ranged along both sides of the Little Missouri River. He built a fine ranch house on a bluff overlooking the river, sent for his wife Medora, and set about his grand plan to transform the beef production system of the United States.

The plan called for the fattening of *his* cattle on *his* range, having them butchered and packed in *his* plant and then shipped east in *his* refrigerated cars on the Northern Pacific. Thus, by cutting out the middlemen, de Mores aimed to produce cheaper beef for the consumer than that provided by the established method of transporting cattle on the hoof by railroad to be processed in the city packing houses. As he rode about his range business the 24-year-old marquis presented a dashing sight, as a correspondent of the *Detroit Free Press* reported:

'He made a picturesque figure in the costume of a plainsman . . . De Mores is tall, well built and graceful. His face is ruddy brown with exposure, with an amiable expression, and certain French characteristics, made more conspicuous by a black moustache and gleaming black eyes . . . A great white hat with a leather band and an immense brim . . . Around his waist was a leather belt filled with gun cartridges; it also held two long-barreled Colt revolvers . . . and a bowie knife . . . His shotgun was double-barreled, made in Paris . . . the arrangements of the locks permitted instant firing.'

The marquis soon demonstrated that he would not hesitate to use his weapons if the situation warranted. When he erected a wire drift fence across an old hunting trail on his land, two hunters named O'Donald and Luffsey cut it down. When de Mores had it repaired they cut it again, regarding it as an illegal restriction on their traditional freedom of movement. Then the Frenchman heard that the two men and a certain 'Dutch' Wannigan had boasted in a saloon that they intended to shoot him. De Mores also received an anonymous note demanding that he leave the territory immediately, or else. It has been said that the trio, being drunk, had voiced empty threats, that they did not really mean to shoot the marquis. That may be so, but the Frenchman took it seriously, and who can blame him?

First, the marquis brought in the law to arrest the men, but when that came to nothing he decided to apprehend the troublesome trio himself. Backed by two of his cowboys, de Mores confronted the hunters and demanded their surrender. It is not clear who started the shooting, but when it ended Luffsey was dead, O'Donald was wounded, and Wannigan had run for his life. When de Mores was accused of murdering Luffsey, a judge ruled that he had acted in self defense. Nobody took the Frenchman lightly after that affair. By the end of 1884 the marquis had established his stock range, packing plant, and a thriving little town with a population of 251; he named the town Medora after his beloved wife.

However, all was not going well for the new enterprise. For various reasons the dressing plant was not processing under full capacity, there were problems with the refrigerator cars, and a shortage of buyers for the meat. His stock herd was mismanaged and when he instructed his agent to buy sheep the man purchased the wrong breed and half of them perished in the winter. The problems piled up, but not the profits. In December 1886 the marquis, having lost some two million dollars, closed down the grand enterprise and returned to France. Ten years later he was killed in a fight with Arab tribesmen in North Africa. The Marquis de Mores was a magnificent failure.

Of all the celebrated cattle kings Richard King was most aptly named. Like a feudal mon-

The Marquis de Mores, the French nobleman who turned to being a Dakota cattleman.

arch of old he carved out a vast domain in southern Texas and held it by force of arms against the attacks of Indians and Mexican brigands. Born in New York in 1825, Richard King ran off to sea at the age of 13 and became a cabin boy. After serving in the Mexican War as a pilot on a government steamer on the Rio Grande, he went into partnership with Captain Mifflin Kenedy and built up a fleet of 22 steamboats.

In 1852 King decided that he wanted a cattle ranch, a ranch that would serve as both business enterprise and family home. Attracted by the unoccupied pastureland watered by the

Santa Gertrudis Creek, southwest of Corpus Christi, King purchased 75,000 acres from the holders of the original Spanish land grants. A man of considerable energy and vision, King invested all the money he could squeeze from his share of the steamboat company into building his ranch and buying livestock. He erected a stockade and a fort, the latter armed with a cannon.

Captain King hired Mexican vaqueros to tend his cattle and horses and induced poor Mexican peasants to leave their villages and come to work for him on the Santa Gertrudis Ranch; here they built new homes and accepted King as their *patrón*, or protector. Firm, just and generous in his treatment of the Mexicans, he won their loyalty and they came to be proud of their appellation, *Los Kineños*—the King People. When Mexican bandits attacked the ranch they met fierce resistance and were driven off. In December 1854 Captain King married Henrietta Chamberlain, daughter of a Presbyterian minister. In the following years the ranch grew and prospered. In 1860 Captain Kenedy became a partner in the venture. Henrietta produced three daughters and two sons, and by 1861 King had 3,000 horses and 20,000 cattle on the range.

King believed in good quality animals and upgraded his beef stock, crossing his native Longhorns with imported blood Durhams. His great love of horses, and the need for trained range mounts, led him to crossbreed Mexican mares with fine Kentucky stallions which resulted in the development of the Western quarter horse, so called for its speed over a quarter mile. Mustangs with a rebel nature did not make good range mounts. To handle cattle required a horse of intelligence, one with 'cow sense,' that could stop, turn, and run at the slightest command. In 1868 Captain King purchased 'blood stallions to improve my horse stock . . . I paid as high as from 300 to 1000 dollars [for each stallion].'

When the Civil War broke out, Richard King, true to his adopted Texas, supported the Confederacy. When the Union Navy blockaded the Southern ports, King's steamboats ferried cotton across the Rio Grande to the Mexican town of Matamoros and brought back much needed British-made arms and ammunition for the Confederate forces. After the war Captain King sent thousands of his cattle on the long drives from Texas to the railheads in Kansas, and to stock the northern ranges. Shrewdly, King hired his boss drovers on a profit-sharing deal,

Below left: Charles Goodnight crossed beef cattle with the buffalo and produced a new species—the cattelo, shown here. It was not a successful breed, however. Below right: A newly branded calf on the Ox Yoke Ranch near Emigrant, Montana.

thus ensuring that his herds reached their destination with the smallest loss of animals. One trail boss named Fitch netted over 5000 dollars in a single drive to Kansas. At one time the 'King of Texas' had livestock holdings that totalled 100,000 cattle and 10,000 horses.

Naturally, such a vast number of animals scattered over 150,000 acres attracted the attention of rustlers and in a six-year period they stole 50,000 head of cattle from Santa Gertrudis. His fine horses were particularly coveted and nearly 1000 were stolen between 1869 and 1872. But such was the continuing growth of his spread that King could endure the loss and still prosper. Juan Cortina, a former general in the Mexican army, was leader of a band of brigands that plagued the region. His depredations had caused many of King's neighbors to abandon their ranches and seek security in nearby towns. But Captain King defied the bandit chief. In March 1875 Cortina's men attacked the Santa Gertrudis Ranch but were driven off by the determined *Kineños*. When Captain King had to make one of his regular business trips between the ranch and Brownsville, 125 miles away, a strong escort of armed cowboys always accompanied his private stagecoach. Once, when the party ran into bandit gunfire, King's

Goodnight is credited with originating the chuck wagon, which became essential to the cowboy's wellbeing on the trail drive and open range roundup.

companion in the coach was killed.

To combat the Mexican outlaw menace, the Texas Rangers were re-formed (they had been disbanded after the Civil War) and a Special Force under Captain McNelly was given the specific task of ridding south Texas of brigands and rustlers, which they did with ruthless efficiency. Captain King continued to expand his ranch and upgrade his livestock. By the time he died in 1885 'King's Kingdom,' as it was called, covered 600,000 acres. The man who took over the reins of this enormous spread was Robert J Kleberg, a young lawyer from Corpus Christi, who had married King's youngest daughter Alice. Under Kleberg's able management the ranch continued to grow and prosper and today the 823,000-acre King Ranch is operated by King-Kleberg descendants. The ranch developed the Santa Gertrudis cattle breed and two Kentucky Derby winners, Assault and Middleground, came from King Ranch thoroughbreds. The city of Kingsville, Kleberg County, was originally built on land which formerly was part of the ranch.

The results of the Dewey-Berry gunfight were three men dead, one man wounded and one horse killed. All of this was triggered over the possession of a five dollar water tank.

6
GUNS AND GUNFIGHTERS

Always have your gun loaded and ready and never reach for it unless you are dead earnest and intend to kill the other fellow.

W B 'Bat' Masterson

One dusty day in 1871 a young Texas trail boss was driving a herd north to Kansas when trouble arose with a Mexican drover, whose herd was crowding close behind, making it difficult to keep the cattle apart. Heated words were exchanged. 'The boss Mexican cursed me,' the young Texan claimed, 'and said he would kill me with a sharp-shooter as quick as he could get it from the wagon.' The Mexican returned with the rifle, dismounted about 100 yards from the Texan, took deliberate aim and fired. The bullet whipped off the Texan's hat and grazed his head. The Mexican pulled the trigger again but the rifle would not fire. He pulled his pistol and signaled his vaqueros to join him.

The young Texan, 18 years old, displaying remarkable coolness under fire, drew his revolver, an old cap-and-ball Colt with a loose cylinder. 'There was so much play between the cylinder and the barrel,' he said, 'that it would not fire unless I held the cylinder with one hand and pulled the trigger with the other.' He dismounted and with the approaching Mexican only ten paces away, he fired the faulty pistol and managed to hit the man in the thigh. The Colt would not fire again and the Texan dashed back to camp, where he obtained the best pistol available and accompanied by another cowboy, he returned to the fight, in which he shot dead the boss Mexican and four of his crew.

The young Texan drover was John Wesley Hardin, who became one of the most notorious gunfighters of frontier history, credited with killing 44 men. His experience with the faulty pistol taught him a lesson he never forgot. He always ensured that his guns were in perfect condition, and always carried two, in case one misfired. Gunfighters rarely, if ever, fired both pistols at the same time in popular Western movie fashion. It seems that Hardin's favorite weapon was Colt's .44 caliber New Model Army of 1860, a six-shot cap-and-ball revolver that was loaded with lead balls and black powder and fired by percussion caps. After 1873 Hardin also used the Colt .45 'Peacemaker' model, the type usually seen in Western films.

The six-shooters produced by Colt's Patent Fire Arms Manufacturing Company of Hartford, Connecticut were the most popular and numerous revolvers of the Old West, used by

working cowboys, gunfighters, lawmen, bandits, and the army. Samuel Colt (1814-62) produced his first model, a five-shot, in 1836 and this found particular favor with the hard riding Texas Rangers in their close and mounted combat with the Comanche Indians. The Colt was the ideal horseman's weapon and the Rangers used it with surprising and devastating effect against the Indians, who were accustomed to dealing with single-shot firearms.

Colt's first six-shot model came in 1847 and because it incorporated certain mechanical suggestions made by Captain Sam Walker of the Texas Rangers it was called the 'Walker' Colt. The US government ordered 1,000 of these heavy .44 caliber revolvers for military use in the Mexican War of 1846-48. The Colt Company produced many different models in the following years. The .36 Navy Model of 1851 was widely used in the American Civil War and by frontiersmen and gunfighters. Wild Bill Hickok carried a pair of Navy Colts. It was called the 'Navy' because .36 was the Navy caliber and the first production models had an engraving on the cylinder depicting a naval battle. The Colt .44 New Model Army of 1860 was the principal revolver used by both Union and Confederate forces in the Civil War, over 200,000 being produced from 1860 to 1873.

The revolver proved essential to the cowboy's survival in a hostile environment. When the occasion demanded he used it against his fellow man; against rattlesnakes, wolves and other four-legged wildlife; to put an injured horse out of its agony; or to drop dangerous cattle. D E McArthur in *The Cattle Industry of Texas, 1865-1918* relates an incident in which a cowboy roping a large and powerful steer was jerked to the ground by the animal and, as he lay trapped under his fallen mount, the steer lowered his sharp horns and charged the prostrate horse and rider:

'It was an awful moment. There appeared no escape . . . Some persons in such a situation would have been paralyzed—would have lost

Opposite top left: John Wesley Hardin. Top right: Hardin's body after being shot dead in 1895. Center: El Paso, Texas in 1895. The man at the toll gate is John Selman, who shot Hardin. Bottom: The Colt .45 'Peacemaker' that is believed to have belonged to John Wesley Hardin.

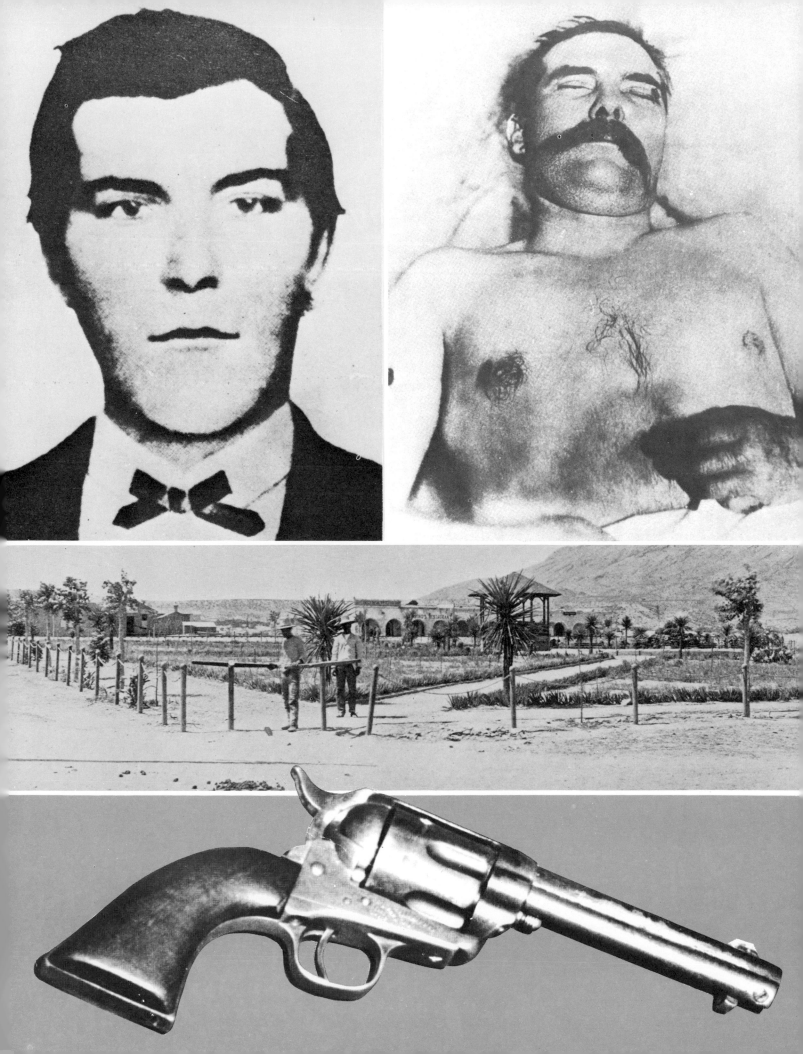

The .36 caliber Texas Paterson model Colt revolver of 1836—a five-shot used by the Texas Rangers.

Another Colt revolver. This is the Colt Navy model six-shooter. It was first manufactured in 1851.

Smith and Wesson revolvers were widely used throughout the cattle country. This is the Model No. 3 of 1870

A Colt .45 caliber 'Peacemaker' made in 1886. This one belonged to Ben Kilpatrick of the Butch Cassidy 'Wild Bunch' gang.

A Walker-Colt revolver manufactured in 1847. This one was one of a pair that belonged to Captain Sam Walker.

The Colt .44 caliber New Model Army of 1860, the most popular revolver used in the Civil War, over 200,000 being produced.

A close rival in popularity to the Colt revolver was the Remington revolver. This is a Remington New Model Army of 1875.

Tom Horn rode the range armed with a Winchester Model 1894. This is a special limited edition that was made in 1977.

all presence of mind. But not so with this young man: his hand was instantly on his revolver, and drawing it he shot the furious animal through the brain, when the delay of a moment would have been fatal.'

Most working cowhands bought their six-shooters over the counter at a gun or hardware store and probably paid little heed to details and to regular maintenance. The ordinary cowboy viewed his handgun as a necessary piece of equipment, to be used when required, but mostly to be worn (especially in town) as a po-tent symbol of his macho calling. Professional gunfighters, however, purchased their firearms with particular attention to detail and took great care of them. Wild Bill Hickok regularly checked the loads of his brace of Navy Colts, cleaning chambers and nipples and inspecting the percussion caps to ensure instant operation. 'When I draw and pull,' he said, 'I must be sure.' Bat Masterson, the celebrated lawman-gunfighter, purchased a total of eight .45 Peace-

A saloon in Albany County, Wyoming. The bartender's Smith and Wesson is stuck in a glass.

maker models directly from the Colt Company during the period 1879-85. He knew exactly what he required in a handgun, as detailed in the following letter he wrote to the company on 24 July 1885:

Gents,

Please send me one of your nickle plated short .45 caliber revolvers. It is for my own use and for that reason I would like to have a little extra paines taken with it. I am willing to pay extra for extra work. Make it very easy on [the] trigger and have the front sight a little higher and thicker than the ordinary pistol of this kind. Put on a gutta percha [hard rubber] handle and send it as soon as possible. Have the barrel about the same length that the ejecting rod is [4¾ inches].
Truly yours
W B Masterson.

The ritualized quick-draw confrontation between rival gunfighters constantly portrayed by Western movie makers, hands poised over six-guns in low-slung holsters, is not historically accurate. Revolvers were worn high on the hip and a gunman intent on killing his rival or victim generally did so covertly, by ambush, trickery or surprise. Shooting a man in the back was far more certain than a risky face-to-face encounter. An experienced man-killer took no chances. Formidable gunfighters such as Hickok, Jesse James, Pat Garrett, and Wes Hardin were all killed by shots in the back, and Billy the Kid was gunned down by surprise in a darkened bedroom. Hickok, however, did engage in a duel somewhat in the Hollywood manner.

It happened on 21 July 1865 in the public square of Springfield, Missouri when Wild Bill faced Dave Tutt, the latter being also a skilled pistol shot. The gunfight was triggered by an argument over a game of poker. Tutt acquired Hickok's watch in the game and boasted that he would wear the timepiece in the town square as a symbol of his triumph. Wild Bill objected to this and said that he would shoot him if he took such action, but Tutt ignored the warning. The two men confronted each other at a distance of 50 yards. Both drew and fired at the same time, or so it appeared to eyewitnesses. Tutt missed with his shot and fell dead with a bullet in the heart. Whereupon Hickok swung round on Tutt's armed friends and leveled his Navy Colt at them, saying: 'Aren't you satisfied, gentlemen? Put up your shooting irons, or there'll be more dead men here.' Suitably impressed by Hickok's marksmanship and cool demeanor, the men dispersed. Bill stood trial for Tutt's death but was acquitted on his plea of self-defense.

According to General George A. Custer Wild Bill was not a 'quarrelsome man, yet no one but himself can enumerate the many conflicts in which he has been engaged and which have almost invariably resulted in the death of his adversary . . . yet he always escapes unhurt . . . Wild Bill always carried two handsome ivory-handled revolvers of the large size; he is never seen without them.'

The guns Custer referred to were probably the silver-plated .36 Navy Colts presented to Hickok by Senator Henry Wilson of Massachusetts as a 'souvenir of the most delightful trip.' In the spring of 1869 Bill had served as scout or guide to Wilson and his party on a visit to the Far West. Hickok had amazed and entertained the party with a display of his shooting skills. It has been claimed that Hickok could cut a chicken's throat with a bullet from 30 paces, without breaking its neck, or touching the head or body; that he could drive the cork into a bottle without breaking the bottle neck, and hit a dime at 50 paces nine times out of ten.

Contrary to what the movies depict, lightning speed in drawing a pistol was not the fundamental requisite of a gunfighter. Of course swiftness in bringing a gun into action was important, but deliberation (which called for cool courage) and accuracy were the prime factors for success. Wyatt Earp commented that deliberation in a shoot-out was the key to survival; the victor, he said, would be the one who 'took his time and pulled the trigger once.' Hickok also advocated that basic rule. 'Whenever you get into a row be sure and not shoot too quick. I've known many a fellow slip up for shooting in a hurry.'

Bat Masterson once gave this advice to a young and inexperienced deputy: 'The main thing is to shoot first and never miss. Never try to run a bluff with a sixgun. Many a man has been buried with his boots on because he

foolishly tried to scare someone by reaching for his hardware . . . So always have your gun loaded and ready, and never reach for it unless you are in dead earnest and intend to kill the other fellow. A lot of inexperienced fellows try to aim a six-shooter by sighting along the barrel, and they try to shoot the other man in the head. Never do that. If you have to stop a man with a gun . . . try to hit him just where the belt buckle would be. That's the broadest target from head to heel.'

Hickok advised the same thing. 'If you have to shoot a man, shoot him in the guts near the navel. You may not make a fatal shot, but he will get a shock that will paralyze his brain and [gun] arm so much that the fight is all over.'

Wild Bill knew all the gunfighting tricks but even he could be taken by surprise, if we are to believe Wes Hardin's autobiography, *The Life of John Wesley Hardin*, 1896. Hickok was marshal of Abilene at the time and Hardin was wearing his guns, in contravention of the town's ordinance. After an initial encounter in which Hickok told Hardin to remove his guns until he was ready to leave town, they had another run-in and Hardin was still wearing guns. Hickok drew his Colt and said: 'Take those pistols off. I arrest you.'

Hardin said 'All right,' pulled out his revolvers and offered them butt-first to Hickok. 'But while he was reaching for them,' Hardin claimed, 'I reversed them and whirled them over on him with the muzzles in his face, springing back at the same time. I told him to put his pistols up, which he did.'

According to Hardin, he cursed Hickok for a 'long haired scoundrel' and then accepted Wild Bill's pacifying invitation to have a drink and talk over the matter. They parted company with a healthy respect for each other but Hardin always believed that 'if Wild Bill [ever] found me in a defenseless condition, he would kill me to add to his reputation.' Later, in May 1874, in the Texas town of Comanche, Hardin himself employed the 'let's have a drink and talk' routine in order to defuse a tense situation. Wes got news that deputy sheriff Charles Webb of Brown County was out to capture or kill

Wild Bill Hickok shoots Dave Tutt, then turns on Tutt's friends with a challenge.

him. When Webb approached him in a saloon Hardin invited him to have a drink. Webb accepted and Hardin led the way to the bar. Somebody shouted, 'Look out!' Wes swung round and, seeing Webb had pulled his gun, leaped aside. Webb fired and the bullet grazed Hardin's side. Wes shot back and the sheriff died with a bullet in the head.

Texas Rangers finally captured Hardin in Pensacola, Florida, in August 1877. Sentenced to 25 years' imprisonment, he was released in 1894. He died with his boots on in August of the following year. It happened in El Paso, Texas. Hardin got into an argument with John Selman, a policeman of the town and a gunman of some repute, with the result that Selman walked up quietly behind Hardin while he was playing dice in a saloon, and shot him dead in the back of the head with a Colt Peacemaker. Selman's claim of shooting in self-defense was upheld. He said that Hardin had threatened to kill him and, 'I wasn't taking any chances.' Not long afterward Selman met his end at the hands of another law officer, as reported by the El Paso *Times* of 6 April 1896:

'John Selman, the victor of not less than 20 shooting affrays in Texas, the exterminator of bad men and the slayer of John Wesley Hardin is dying tonight with a bullet hole through his body. About three months ago Selman and deputy United States Marshal George Scarborough had a quarrel over a game of cards. Since which occurrence the relations between them have been none too cordial. This morning at four o'clock they met at the Wigwam Saloon and both were drinking.'

They left the saloon and shots were fired in an alley. Scarborough stood trial and was acquitted. But such was the gunfighting syndrome that Scarborough himself was killed in a shoot-out in April 1900 with Bill Carver of Butch Cassidy's 'Wild Bunch' gang. A year later Carver was killed by lawmen in Arizona.

With the perfection of the metallic cartridge—in which percussion cap, powder and ball were contained in a single metal case—firearms manufacture was revolutionized and a whole new line of Colt revolvers was produced, of which the .45 Single Action Army Model of 1873, also known as the Peacemaker model, became the most famous and enduring. It is still in production today, a favorite with collectors and target shooters. With a single action wea-

Top: A gallery of gunfighters photographed in Dodge City in June 1883. Back row left to right: W H Harris, Luke Short, Bat Masterson, W F Petillon. Front row: Charlie Basset, Wyatt Earp, M F McLean, Neil Brown.

Above: A Colt .45 'Buntline Special.' This is the type of revolver that Ned Buntline is said to have given to Earp.

pon the hammer is hand-cocked, usually by the thumb, for each shot; with a double-action or self-cocking revolver a single pull on the trigger both cocked and fired the gun.

The Peacemaker was produced in a variety of calibers and barrel lengths: standard lengths being 4¾ inches, 5½ inches, and 7½ inches. But some Peacemakers were made with extra-long barrels, up to 16 inches in length. When the Colt Company first introduced its unusual long-barreled .45 revolver in 1876 it was known as 'Colt's pistol with carbine barrel and attachable stock,' the stock being the metal skeleton type.

It was not a popular model and Colt produced a very small number during the frontier years. The appellation 'Buntline Special'—for a Peacemaker with a 12-inch barrel—was first coined by journalist Stuart N Lake in his controversial biography *Wyatt Earp: Frontier Marshal* in 1931. It was this book, largely discredited in recent years by serious historians, that estab-

Above: The Gunfight at the OK Corral as depicted on a poster for the film *Hour of the Gun*, 1967.

Below: Another scene of the OK Corral gunfight. James Garner is Earp; Jason Robards is Doc.

114

lished the legendary fame and supposed exploits of Wyatt Earp.

Lake tells us that Ned Buntline (pseudonym of Edward Zane Carroll Judson), the dime novel fiction writer, ordered five special .45 Peacemakers with 12-inch barrels from the Colt

Tom Horn, the man-hunting range detective, as photographed while he was awaiting his trial on charges of murder.

Company and presented them in the summer of 1876 to the Western peace officers he most admired, including Wyatt Earp, Bat Masterson, and Bill Tilghman. According to Lake, the so-called Buntline Special became Earp's favorite weapon and he would often use the long barrel to club troublemakers senseless. However, the other recipients of the Buntlines found the long barrels inconvenient and cut them down to standard length.

It is now clear that Earp never carried a Buntline Special, a truth fully established by William B Shillingberg's brilliant monograph *Wyatt Earp and the 'Buntline Special' Myth* published in The Kansas Historical Quarterly, Summer 1976. Shillingberg informs us that there is no mention of the alleged Ned Buntline order

in the Colt Company's carefully preserved records, that no long-barreled Peacemakers left the factory until December 1876, and that there is no mention of the name 'Buntline Special' in writings that predate Lake's book. Of course, Earp's giant gun was said to have been lost many years ago. It was not until 1957 that the Colt Company decided to exploit the legendary publicity attached to the weapon (stimulated at the time by the TV series *Wyatt Earp*) and started using the official designation 'Buntline Special' for its long-barreled Peacemaker, which is still produced today.

It was in the Arizona town of Tombstone that the West's most celebrated and dramatized shoot-out, the 'Gunfight at the OK Corral,' took place on 26 October 1881 between the Earp brothers, aided by 'Doc' Holliday, and the Clanton-McLaury cowboy faction.

It is not certain what type of handgun Wyatt used in the fight at the OK Corral. Some experts say it was a .44 Smith & Wesson 'American' model of 1869, others claim it was a Peacemaker of standard length. Actually, the shoot-out did not take place in the OK Corral but on Fremont Street, at the rear of the corral. For many years this gunfight was generally understood to be a showdown between the law, represented by the Earps, and a bunch of badmen. Some of the people of Tombstone at the time held another view. 'To be plain,' said an eye-witness named Lewis, 'it was simply a fight between stage-robbers, and was getting rid of a lot of bad eggs on both sides, the good citizens said nothing and let it go on.'

After serving as a policeman in Wichita, Kansas, and then as assistant marshal of Dodge City, Wyatt and his brothers Virgil and Morgan, together with John Henry 'Doc' Holliday moved to Tombstone, where they were known as the Earp gang. Virgil became the town marshal and Wyatt worked as a shotgun messenger with a stagecoach company. Trouble had been brewing for some time between the Earps and the Clanton-McLaury cowboy faction. The brothers Ike and Billy Clanton and Tom and Frank McLaury (sometimes spelled McLowery) had reputations as rustlers. Intent on settling matters between the rival parties once and for all, Virgil Earp took the precaution of deputizing his brothers and Holliday and at about two o'clock on the afternoon of 26 October 1881 the Earps and the deadly dentist marched along Fremont Street toward the assembled Clanton-McLaury brothers and their friend Billy Claibourne. Sheriff John Behan attempted to stop the Earps but they brushed him aside; they were intent on a showdown.

Eyewitness accounts differ in many ways. Some said that the Earps opened fire without just cause, others claim that they shot in self-defense. The fight was over in less than a minute. Both sides had fired at close range. The two McLaury boys and Billy Clanton were shot dead. Virgil and Morgan Earp were wounded; Holliday suffered a slight injury and Wyatt emerged unscathed. Wyatt and Holliday were arrested on murder warrants made out by sheriff Behan and Ike Clanton. At the preliminary hearing in Tombstone, Justice Wells Spicer absolved the accused of murder, saying they had 'been fully justified in committing these homicides.' But the affair did not end there. Several weeks later Virgil Earp was crippled for life when an unknown person fired a shotgun at him. In March 1882 Morgan Earp was killed by a shot in the back while playing billiards in a saloon; Wyatt soon after shot a man suspected of Morgan's murder.

Clay Allison was a 'shootist' (his own term) widely feared and respected in several Western states, credited with killing 15 men. Born in

Tennessee, Robert Clay Allison served a short hitch in a Confederate regiment during the Civil War, his unstable, often violent character

Below: Clay Allison recovering from a shooting in 1870. Bottom: Allison killing John 'Chunk' Colbert.

bringing him a medical discharge. He went to Texas and worked as a cowboy, riding herd for Charles Goodnight. By 1870 he had his own ranch in Colfax County, New Mexico. Legend has it that Allison was a wild man when the worse for drink, a roaring, swaggering braggart. But R D. Gage who knew him in Pecos, Texas, recalled him differently:

'When he came into town he laid aside his ranch clothes and would frequently appear dressed from head to foot in black broadcloth. When sober he was a quiet, pleasant, affable man, but when under the influence of liquor he was a very dangerous man with whom to come in contact. He was never boisterous or loud spoken. In fact, the drunker he became, the softer became his speech, dropping down almost to a whisper.'

Legend also has it that Allison tangled with noted lawmen Wyatt Earp and Bat Masterson but there is little substance in such tales. Just exactly how many men Clay killed, and in what circumstances is open to argument. Bill Oden in *Early Days on the Texas-New Mexico Plains* records his impression of Allison, the shootist:

'I remember him quite well . . . a quiet, unassuming man with no element of the desperado about him. He never killed anyone except in self-defense, but he had about one dozen to his credit, all of whom needed killing for the good of society. The badmen were always hunting him and we expected he would eventually die with his boots on . . . He once told me that he was not a good shot at a mark, except when the mark was a bad man. He seemed to think that he had just been simply lucky.'

Good fortune sided with Allison in his gunfight with John 'Chunk' Colbert at the Clifton House Inn, Cimarron, New Mexico on 7 January 1874. Colbert was the nephew of a man who had lost a fight with Allison a few years previously and was out to even the score. The two men exchanged heated words and sized each other up for several hours, trying to 'get the drop' on the other. Both men sat down to eat at the same table. Allison laid his pistol on the table beside his plate. Colbert held his gun, fully cocked, in his lap. Moments later, Colbert made a grab for Allison's weapon with his left hand, at the same time that he attempted to fire

A poster for one of the more realistic cowboy films, *Tom Horn*, starring Steve McQueen.

his own pistol. But his pistol struck the table and fired without injuring Allison. Before Colbert could shoot again, Clay blew his brains out.

On 1 November 1875 Allison, again in self-defense, killed noted gunman Francisco Griego in the St James Hotel, Cimarron, when the Mexican confronted him over the death of a friend. In 1876 Clay and his brother John were celebrating Christmas at the Olympic Dance Hall in Las Animas, Colorado, when a disturbance brought deputy sheriff Charles Faber to the scene. Armed with a shotgun, Faber opened fire and wounded John Allison. Clay drew his pistol and killed the lawman with his first bullet. Clay was charged with manslaughter but did not stand trial as no witnesses chose to appear in court. Clay Allison died with his boots on, but not by a bullet. In July 1887 he was driving a wagon-load of supplies to his ranch when he fell off (some say in a drunken state) and one of the wagon wheels ran over his head, killing him.

As ubiquitous as Colt's six-shooters were the repeating rifles produced by the Winchester Company of New Haven, Connecticut. Called 'the Gun that won the West,' the Winchester was the most popular general purpose rifle of the time. It was so popular that Colt chambered its Peacemaker model of 1878 to take the same .44-40 cartridge as that used in the Winchester Model 1873 in order that frontiersmen need carry just one type of ammunition; this .44-40 Colt was called the 'Frontier' model. The town of Winchester, Idaho, was so named in 1888 when the town founders decided that the place would be called after whichever gun was carried by the most people present. The Winchester 1873, the type usually seen in cowboy movies, was the most widely used by Westerners, a total of 720,610 being produced up to 1919 when manufacture of the model was discontinued.

Oliver F. Winchester (1810-80), a shirt manufacturer, established himself in the firearms business in 1857 when he purchased the assets of the Volcanic Repeating Arms Company, which had produced pistols and rifles featuring a special repeating mechanism actuated by a trigger-guard lever. Winchester organized a new company called The New Haven Arms Company and made Benjamin T Henry, a highly-skilled gun mechanic, the superintendent of the

A modern advertisement intended to publicize Winchester rifles, especially the Model 1866.

plant. In 1858 Henry devised a self-contained metal-cased rim-fire cartridge and developed a rifle—based on the Volcanic Arms system—to fire it. The successful Henry rifle, as it was called, housed 15 cartridges in a tubular magazine under the barrel; it was operated by moving the trigger-guard lever down and back to its original position, a swift, simple movement that extracted the spent cartridge, moved a fresh shell from the spring-activated magazine into the chamber, and cocked the hammer ready for firing.

In 1866 Oliver Winchester reorganized his firearms business as the Winchester Repeating Arms Company and produced a new improved version of the Henry, called the Winchester rifle, Model 1866. The second Winchester, the Model of 1873, was basically the same as the earlier model but was stronger, simpler, and lighter. It had a sliding lid covering the ejection port in the top of the frame to keep dirt and water out of the action; the frame and butt plate were of forged iron (later of steel) to replace the brass of the Model 1866. It used a .44-40 center-fire cartridge (.44 caliber bullet and 40 grains of powder) which gave a substantial increase in range and stopping power over the earlier model's .44 rimfire cartridge of 28 grains.

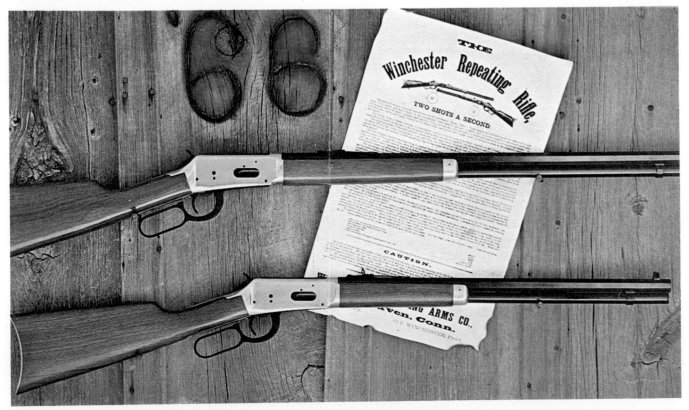

Buffalo Bill Cody was full of praise for the Winchester 1873 and wrote the following letter to the company in 1875: 'I have been using and have thoroughly tested your latest improved rifle. I pronounce your improved Winchester THE BOSS. Believe me that you have the MOST COMPLETE rifle ever made.' Cody was armed with 'the boss' when he engaged in his celebrated duel with Cheyenne chief Yellow Hand in July 1876 during his service as an army scout. Cody describes the fight in his autobiography.

'The chief was riding his horse to and fro in front of his men, in order to banter me. I concluded to accept his challenge. I turned and galloped toward him for fifty yards, and he rode toward me about the same distance. Both of us rode at full speed. When we were only thirty yards apart I raised my rifle and fired. His horse dropped dead under him, and he rolled over on the ground to clear himself of the carcass. Almost at the same instant my own horse stepped into a hole and fell heavily. The fall hurt me but little and almost instantly I was on my feet . . . The chief and I were now both on our feet, not twenty paces apart. We fired at each other at the same instant. My usual luck held. His bullet whizzed harmlessly past my head, while mine struck him full in the breast.'

Cody then scalped the dead Yellow Hand. Lifting the gory trophy high for the benefit of the watching soldiers, he shouted, 'The first scalp for Custer!' (Custer had been killed a few weeks earlier.) Yellow Hand had been armed with a Winchester 1866, a model much prized among Indians for its gleaming brass frame. The Model 1894 was the first sporting repeating-action rifle on the market that was designed for cartridges loaded with smokeless powder. The .30-30 caliber 1894 became a world-wide success with sportsmen and hunters, more than four million being sold over the years. Tom Horn, range detective, carried a .30-30 Winchester during his lone hunting trips. But Horn was not after deer.

Tom Horn, cowboy, former army scout and

Buffalo Bill's duel with the Cheyenne chief Yellowhand by Charles M Russell. Both used Winchester rifles.

Pinkerton agent, became a professional gunman in the most proper sense of the word. Hired by prominent Wyoming cattlemen to protect their stock against rustlers, Horn rode the range alone, trailing cattle and horse thieves; a crack shot with a rifle, Horn killed the men instead of arresting them. It is claimed that he charged 500 dollars for each rustler he shot. A close-mouthed loner by nature, he would, however, talk indiscreetly when deep in drink. 'Killing men is my specialty,' he once divulged. 'I see it as a business and I reckon I have a corner in the trade.' Although it was never proved that he gunned down alleged rustlers, his reputation as a deadly man-hunter was such that by 1898 cattle stealing in Wyoming had been reduced to its lowest level ever. And it was chiefly his reputation as a hired killer that led to his legal execution.

Tom Horn learned to track men as an army scout in the Apache campaigns of the 1880s. Later he served as deputy under sheriff Bucky O'Neil of Yavapai County, Arizona. While working for O'Neil, Tom trailed two outlaws, caught up with them and in the ensuing gunfight killed one but was badly wounded himself. The hunter became the hunted. He crawled into the brush with the surviving outlaw searching for him. Horn, suffering his injury silently, waited with revolver at the ready as his pursuer approached. When the man found him, Horn shot him dead. He had just sufficient strength left to haul himself into the saddle and ride for help.

Horn also worked as a cowboy, a top hand noted for his steer-roping skill. In the 4 July 1888 rodeo at Globe, Arizona, he set a record for roping and tying a steer. From 1890 to 1894 he served as a Pinkerton agent and captured a number of robbers. As an honest cowboy his sympathies always sided with the cattleman against the rustler. He set himself up as a freelance range or stock detective and was highly regarded by those who hired him. 'Tom Horn,' said one rancher, 'had the honorable trait never to peach on [inform against] accomplices or employers. He classed cattle thieves with wolves and coyotes and looked upon himself as a benefactor of society in destroying them, killing without feeling or compunction when certain he was after a guilty man.'

Horn the hunter went about his deadly business armed with a .30-30 Winchester, a pair of powerful binoculars, and a .45 Model 1878 double-action Colt; he carried the revolver in an army style flap holster, more concerned with the gun's protection than a fast draw. When Willie Nickell, 14-year-old son of sheep rancher Kels Nickell, was found shot dead in 1901, rumor and reputation pointed the finger at Tom Horn. Sheep were anathema to cattlemen. It would appear that Horn, lying in wait for Kels Nickell, shot his son by mistake in the dim dawn light, for the boy, big for his age, was wearing his father's coat and hat and was riding his father's horse. Then again the assassin might have been a member of the Miller family; the Millers and the Nickells hated each other and Jim Miller had once tried to kill Kels Nickell with a knife. Horn maintained to the end that he never murdered the boy.

The main evidence against Horn was his 'confession,' tricked out of him by deputy US Marshal Joe LeFors. While Horn was under the influence of drink in LeFors' office, a stenographer concealed in an adjoining room wrote down Horn's so-called confession as LeFors talked to Horn about the murder. When Horn, at his trial, denied the confession and questioned its content, the stenographer, Mr Ohnhaus, was asked by the judge: 'Is that a full and complete reproduction of the conversation?'

Ohnhaus replied: 'Well, I didn't take it all down. I took down all I thought was essential.' Not surprisingly, the trial at Cheyenne, Wyoming, was a controversial one. Many thought, and still do, that Horn was innocent of this particular killing.

The jury found him guilty and he was sentenced to hang. An appeal was lodged. Then Horn got weary of waiting to hear if he would live or die and managed to escape from the jail, taking his guard's Luger automatic pistol. Shot at by the pursuing townsfolk and lawmen, Horn did not shoot back. It is said that he leveled the gun as if to fire but did not do so. He was recaptured quickly and returned to jail. It appears that Horn had not put the Luger's safety catch all the way off. He was hanged on 20 November 1903 while two brothers sang *Life's Railroad to Heaven*; strangely appropriate, for many believed that Tom Horn, condemned by his gunman reputation, had certainly been 'railroaded' to the gallows.

The Rocky Mountains: Emigrants Crossing the Plains by Currier and Ives, 1866.

7
RANGE WARS

Oh beat the drum slowly and play the fife lowly,
And play the dead march as you bear me along;
In the green valley, lay the sod o'er me,
For I'm a poor cowboy and know I've done wrong.
The Streets of Laredo, old cowboy lament

John H Tunstall, enterprising son of a London banker, arrived in New Mexico in 1876 intent on making his mark as a prominent businessman in Lincoln County. He secured a ranch on the Feliz River, some 40 miles south of Lincoln town, stocked it with 500 cattle purchased from John Chisum, and hired some young cowhands and a ranch foreman, Dick Brewer. With financial aid from Chisum and partnered by lawyer Alexander McSween, Tunstall opened a store and bank building in Lincoln, in opposition to the established store, known as 'The House,' run by L G Murphy and his associates. The Murphy faction resented Tunstall's trade incursion; a bitter rivalry developed that resulted in the murder of Tunstall while he was out riding in February 1878, a cold-blooded act that sparked off the Lincoln County range war and launched Billy the Kid, one of Tunstall's cowboys, into legendary orbit.

The Lincoln County conflict was but one of many range wars, major and minor, that plagued the cattle country. It was usually the cowboys on the one side versus the hated sheepmen, homesteaders, grangers, and rustlers, the latter being for the most part, in cattlemen's prejudiced eyes, any little rancher or ambitious cowboy with a small herd. The cattle kings, well organized and powerful, had smart lawyers and armed riders to secure and enforce their claims and demands over disputed grazing land, most of it being public domain to which they had no proper legal title. The newcomers, however, increasing in numbers and determined to have their share of the Great Plains, challenged the entrenched cattlemen and a long struggle ensued for control of the land. A lot of blood stained the prairies before the issue was resolved in favor of the homesteader.

The Lincoln County War was essentially a conflict between business interests. During its six-month course 19 men were killed in the shooting and many were wounded. Murphy and his associates had a good thing going with The House. They had contracts to supply beef to the Indian reservations and to military posts. They purchased cattle from small ranchers at low prices and sold goods at inflated prices to the settlers. Their firm grip on the county was strengthened by political friends in the territo-

rial capital of Santa Fe and they controlled the county sheriff, William Brady. Cattle king John Chisum was convinced that the Murphy mob was stealing his stock. Tunstall's arrival and the popularity of the new store threatened to undermine the Murphy organization.

Billy the Kid, then known as William Bonney, aged about 18, had been hired by Tunstall

William 'Billy the Kid' Bonney, the ruthless killer. The photograph was probably taken in 1880.

Below: Billy was killed in July 1881. This 'true life' was published in the following August. Bottom: Billy being shot dead by Pat Garrett in Pete Maxwell's bedroom.

THE FIVE CENT

WIDE AWAKE LIBRARY

No. 451. COMPLETE. FRANK TOUSEY, PUBLISHER, 20 ROSE STREET, N.Y. New York, August 29, 1881. Issued Every Monday. PRICE 5 CENTS. Vol. I.

TRUE LIFE OF BILLY THE KID

despite the Kid's previous association with the Murphy faction. This act of trust greatly impressed Billy and he gave his loyalty to the man. 'John Tunstall was the only friend I ever had, besides my mother,' the Kid told Mrs. McSween, wife of the Englishman's partner. 'He gave me my first real job. And when I started work he gave me a new saddle and a fine horse.' On Tunstall's death, it is said, Billy vowed vengeance against the killers. What the Kid lacked in physical build he more than made up with reckless courage, skill with firearms, and a ruthless killer streak.

On the first day of March Dick Brewer, appointed special deputy by Justice Wilson of Lincoln, headed a posse that included Billy.

Below: A photograph of Pat Garrett, the sheriff who shot and killed Billy the Kid, 1881.

The homesteaders arrive in this painting by
H Charles McBarron, *Oklahoma Land Rush of 1889.*

They pursued a group of men involved in Tunstall's murder and captured two of them, named Morton and Baker. What happened on the way back to Lincoln is confused. There was shooting, one of the posse fell dead, and suddenly Morton and Baker were galloping off. Billy spurred the horse that Tunstall had given him and gave chase. He gained ground on them and when he was about 100 yards away, pulled up sharp, jerked his Winchester out of its scabbard and dismounted. Taking careful aim he fired twice, killing both men.

A month later Sheriff Brady with two deputies, Hindman and Peppin, left the Murphy store to walk to the courthouse. All were armed. They were fired on by a group behind an adobe wall; the ambushers included Billy the Kid. Brady was killed instantly and Hindman mortally wounded. Peppin took cover and returned the fire, inflicting a wound on Billy. The next shootout, a few weeks later, involved Dick Brewer and his posse and a man named 'Buckshot Bill' Roberts. This man had nothing to do with Tunstall's murder but he had connections with the Murphy faction, and there was bad blood between him and Charlie Bowdre, a member of the posse. That seemed reason enough to 'go for him' at a settlement called Blazer's Mill. They caught a tartar in Buckshot Bill.

Having received a mortal wound from Bowdre, Roberts shot one of his attackers through the body and another in the gun hand, he then staggered to a building where he holed up, dying. Despite his dreadful condition, the gutsy Buckshot could still shoot straight. When Dick Brewer decided to flush him out and exposed himself to get off some shots at the doorway, Roberts put a bullet in the middle of Brewer's forehead. That was enough for the others; with their leader dead, they rode off and left their victim to die in his own time. George Peppin, sympathetic to the Murphy cause, was made sheriff of Lincoln County and he pressed the action against McSween, which culminated in a three-day gun battle in the town of Lincoln.

Peppin, with a strong force, besieged McSween and his supporters, including Billy the Kid, in the McSween home. The battle came to an end on the night of 19 July 1878 when the McSween house was set alight. As the lawyer

Opposite top left: The aftermath of a lynching; an unidentified victim hanged near Prescott, Arizona in the 1880s. Top right: Vigilantes returning from a lynching in the Old West (engraving by Rufus Zogbaum). Bottom left: The lynching of 'Cattle Kate' Watson and James Averill, Wyoming, 1889. Bottom right: A photograph of an early sheepherder taken on the western plains.

and some others walked out of the burning building to surrender they were shot down without mercy, the unarmed McSween dying with a Bible in his hand. Billy displayed more spunk and sense; he made a break for it, shooting on the run, and he got clean away.

With the chief protagonists now dead or dying (Murphy succumbed to an illness in October 1878) the war was virtually over. Major General Lew Wallace took office as Governor of New Mexico on 1 October and, in an attempt to stop the trouble completely, he proclaimed an amnesty for all those involved in the bloody feud. But negotiations with Billy the Kid went sour, John Chisum turned against him, and the Kid became an outlaw; he was eventually shot dead in 1881 by the new sheriff of Lincoln County, Pat Garrett, who had not taken part in the conflict.

The sheep invasion of the open range caused great bitterness and bloodshed. Cattlemen feared and despised sheep and sheepmen. And in their view they had just cause. They claimed that the hated animals ruined the grass by eating it too close and destroyed even the roots with their massed, sharp hoofs, creating barren regions on the open range. Cowboys maintained that sheep left a stink on the land and in watering places that upset cattle and horses. Julian Ralph in an article on Wyoming in *Harper's New Monthly Magazine* of June 1893 quotes a cattleman thus:

'The sheep-herder is the worst blot on the State. He is no good, and much harm . . . He fits out a wagon, with a Mexican and a dog and several thousand sheep, and away they go, like an Egyptian scourge, eating the grass down to the ground, and in sandy soils, trampling it down so that there are great regions where once the bunch-grass grew knee-high, but where the country is now bare as a desert.'

The cowboy, the mounted pioneer of the plains, viewed the newly arrived, pedestrian

Range wars were common in the 1880s, usually between nesters and groups of vigilantes. This illustration by Rufus F. Zogbaum is The Vigilantes, showing an incident in the range wars.

Cowboys considered the sheep rancher to be a mortal enemy. In this drawing the cowboys are out for blood. They are raiding a sheepherder's camp and slaughtering his flock.

sheep-herder (rarely referred to as a shepherd) with utter contempt, a contempt compounded by the fact that many of the sheep-herders were Mexican or Indian or white men of recent foreign origin—Basque, French and German. And the solitary life, the constant bleating of their flocks, drove many herders insane. They were, it seems, a strange breed of men. Cattlemen, by virtue of being there first and having established 'ownership' of a particular part of open range, determined to hold what they had by force of arms. But the free range was government land, its ownership by individuals restricted by laws. Nevertheless, cattlemen took to promulgating 'deadlines,' boundaries that sheepmen were warned not to cross; they did so at their peril. But the stubborn sheepmen wanted their share of the free grass and kept right on coming.

Cowboys attacked the sheep herds, usually at night, with their faces masked. They would slaughter the sheep in great numbers, and beat or kill the herders, depending on the mood of the moment and if the herder resisted. They would set fire to his covered wagon and tie his dogs to the wheels. The sheep were shot, clubbed, burned or blown up with dynamite; a favorite method of extermination was driving a herd over a high cliff. The sheepmen fought back and on the Wyoming-Colorado range some 20 men died in the fighting, hundreds were injured, and 600,000 sheep were destroyed. Cowboys committed many awful deeds in order to keep the sheepmen out of the cattle country. But the sheep kept on coming, like the homesteader, and the days of the cattle kings were numbered. A new West was in the making.

Sheep exacerbated a family feud in Arizona known as the Pleasant Valley War: a series of retaliatory killings that lasted for five years and resulted, perhaps, in 50 deaths, the exact figure is uncertain. The chief protagonists were the Tewksbury and Graham families. Pleasant Valley, 50 miles long, well watered and richly grassed lay beneath the high peaks of the Mogollon Rim in a secluded corner of Apache County. In the early 1880s it was occupied by cattlemen, who, knowing that sheep were appearing on the ranges to the north, had designated the Mogollons as the deadline, and the

sheepmen acknowledged the boundary.

Among the first to settle in the valley were the Tewksbury brothers, Edwin, John, and Jim, halfbreed sons of a New Englander and his Indian wife. They ran a small horse ranch. A few years later the Graham brothers, Tom, John, and Billy, came to the valley and established a small cattle herd. At first the two families were friendly, then they fell out and there developed a lasting acrimony between them. When Mart Blevins and his five sons arrived in the valley from Texas early in 1884 to set up a modest cattle ranch, the Blevins allied themselves to the Grahams.

The small herd of the Grahams grew rapidly, and as other ranchers had been steadily losing cattle, it was suspected that the Grahams were stealing livestock to increase their own herd. Tewksbury horses were also being stolen and they accused the Grahams and their friends, who included the Blevins and the cowboys of the Aztec Land and Cattle Company, known locally as the Hashknife outfit from the design of its brand. Andy Blevins, who it seems was essentially a bad man, had changed his name to Cooper because he was wanted for rustling in Texas and Oklahoma. The Tewksburys called the Grahams thieves, the Grahams responded by calling the halfbreed brothers 'red niggers' and threatened to run them out of the valley.

In February, 1887 Hashknife cowboys reported that sheep were being driven over the Mogollon deadline into the valley. The sheep were owned by the Daggs brothers of Flagstaff who, desperate for fresh grazing, had decided to break the previously respected deadline. The sheep were driven by a Basque, two Indian helpers, and William Jacobs, the latter being a friend of the Tewksburys. Cowboys killed the Basque and ran the sheep over a cliff; the other herders escaped and sought protection at the Tewksbury ranch.

A few months later Mart Blevins, out riding, disappeared, and his sons accused the Tewksburys of his murder. Early in August, Hampton Blevins and four Hashknife riders came upon Ed and Jim Tewksbury in a cabin and a gunfight ensued in which Hampton and a cowboy were shot dead and the other Hashknife men put to flight, all of them wounded. The Tewksburys emerged from the encounter unscathed.

A week later Billy Graham, youngest of the brothers, was shot dead while riding alone. His killer, James Houck, was an acknowledged Tewksbury partisan.

On the morning of 2 September a Graham-Blevins party approached the Tewksbury ranch and caught John Tewksbury and Jacobs, the sheep herder, in the open. The raiders shot both men dead and lay siege to the ranch, which was stoutly defended by Ed and Jim and their father for several days until the attackers gave up and departed. A few days after the siege Andy (Blevins) Cooper turned up at the town of Holbrook on a family visit. He openly boasted about killing a Tewksbury and his reputation as a rustler was well known. Under pressure from local ranchers the newly elected sheriff of Apache County, Commodore Perry Owens (named after the naval hero of the War of 1812), set out to arrest Cooper.

Armed with a sixgun and a Winchester rifle, Owens knocked on the door of the house in which Cooper was staying with his two brothers John and Sam, a friend named Roberts and some women. When the door was opened Owens found himself facing an armed Andy and John. The sheriff ordered Andy to come with him; he refused, and the shooting began. Cooper went down, mortally wounded in the belly. John fired and missed Owens, who, shooting his Winchester from the hip, struck John in the shoulder and put him out of action. The sheriff then stepped back into the street to cover both sides of the house. When Roberts, gun in hand, came through the window, Owens hit him with a fatal bullet. That left young Sam, 16 years old. Mad with grief and anger he grabbed Andy's pistol and ran out of the front door to be shot dead by the waiting lawman.

This latest ramification of the Tewksbury-Graham feud galvanized the territorial governor to order William Mulvenon, sheriff of Yavapai County, to muster a large posse and sweep through Pleasant Valley in order to suppress the spreading war. Mulvenon set out to arrest the leading participants of both sides. When John Graham and Charles Blevins rode into the sheriff's net on 21 September, Mulvenon leveled a shotgun at them and demanded their surrender. In reply they spurred their mounts and drew their guns. Mulvenon blasted

Blevins from his saddle, while the posse shot down Graham; both men died. When the sheriff rode to the Graham ranch, Tom Graham and his gunmen were gone. Mulvenon then went to the Tewksbury place and arrested Ed and Jim, who submitted quietly and were soon out on bond. Mulvenon later arrested Tom Graham in Phoenix.

When the three men were indicted and brought to trial, no witnesses could be found willing to testify and the charges were dropped. The partisan killings continued, mostly vigilante lynchings of Graham adherents, that is, suspected rustlers. On 1 August 1892 Tom Graham was shot dead while driving his wagon on the trail; some children who witnessed the shooting identified the killers as Ed Tewksbury and John Rhodes. Both were arrested and stood trial for murder. In court, Anne Graham, Tom's widow, drew her husband's sixgun from her umbrella, pressed it into Rhodes' back and pulled the trigger. But the gun failed to fire, and before she could try again the avenging widow was seized and hurried out of the courtroom. Rhodes provided an alibi for the time of the murder and was acquitted. Ed Tewksbury was found guilty, won an appeal and was eventually released in February, 1895. The sole survivor of the family feud, brother Jim having died of tuberculosis in 1888, Ed succumbed to the same disease in 1904.

The Johnson County War of 1892 was a clash of arms and will power between the wealthy, influential cattlemen of the Wyoming Stock Growers Association and the grangers, or small independent ranchers and farmers, and the nesters who, in ever increasing numbers, were staking claims and breaking up the cattle country. 'Nester' was the derogatory cowboy name for a homesteader, whose cabin, with its feed patch encircled by protective brushwood, looked from a distance like a huge bird's nest. The big cattlemen viewed these humble newcomers as enemies of the open range and equated them with rustlers. The difference in social standing and ownership between the two

parties were clearly defined in the *Golden Era* newspaper of White Oaks, New Mexico, 8 May 1884:

'The nester . . . is the cattle king's neighbor. Between them there is a wide gap in rank. A man may own a section of land and have 50 to 100 or 200 head of cattle, but he is only a nester . . . His land is a "farm" and his stock "a bunch." When he counts his pasture owned or leased by the section instead of by the acre, then he has got a "range," and when his stock is counted by the thousand instead of by the head, then he has a herd. There is a genuine cowman. He joins a livestock association. He has a brand known and recognized . . . When he goes to the cities the papers refer to him as Mr So-and-So, the cattle king.'

By 1890, in northern Wyoming, the homesteaders had acquired political power and controlled Johnson County. South of the county the cattlemen, based in Cheyenne, reigned supreme and controlled much of the political power of the state. Most of the nesters and grangers of Johnson County were honest, hardworking folk, but there were among them maverick cowboys who were stealing livestock from the big cattle companies in order to establish a herd of their own. The injured cattlemen maintained that the Johnson County authorities

A scene from *Heaven's Gate*. Nate Champion fights back.

were in sympathy with the 'rustler community' and that it was impossible to have them prosecuted. So the cattlemen decided to handle the matter in their own ruthless manner (as, indeed, they always had done).

They hired range detectives to spy on the nesters to find evidence of stock thieving; they paid assassins to murder known rustlers, and they carried out vigilante lynchings. Perhaps some of the lynchings were justified, according to the rough and ready 'Code of the West,' but surely not the hanging of Ella Watson. Ella was a whore from Kansas who lived in a little settlement on the Sweetwater range south of Johnson County, and she sometimes accepted cattle in lieu of payment from her cowboy customers. James Averill, Ella's neighbor and friend, ran a small saloon and store; he was an educated man and wrote articles for the Casper *Weekly Mail* denouncing the monopolistic power and land grabbing greed of the cattle kings. In July, 1889 masked men dragged Ella and Averill from their cabins and hanged them. In an effort to justify this dreadful deed the cattlemen spread the word that the unfortunate whore was in fact 'Cattle Kate,' a notorious rustler queen.

The final threat to the monopoly of the Wyoming Stock Growers Association (formed in 1873 in Cheyenne) came with the formation early in 1892 of the rival Northern Wyoming Farmers and Stock Growers Association, which announced the intention of holding its own independent round-up, and named two foremen of the coming event, one being a Texan, Nathan 'Nate' Champion, a top cowhand and a gunfighter of some note. Assassins hired by the cattlemen had previously made an attempt on Champion's life in a cabin on the Powder River but Nate had driven them off, wounding two in the process.

The announcement of the rival association was the final slap in the face for the cattle

Below: Frank Canton, a leading participant in the Johnson County War of 1892. Bottom: The cabin on the KC Ranch in which Nate Champion was besieged by the invaders.

kings. A cabal was held at the luxurious Cheyenne Club and a decision was made to invade Johnson County and wipe out all known and suspected rustlers once and for all. A death list with 75 names was drawn up. To implement this extermination project, 25 Texas gunfighters were hired to supplement a local force of 'Regulators,' the leaders being Frank Wolcott, an ex-army major and now a cattleman, and Frank Canton, a professional gunman with a sinister past. A number of prominent politicians were privy to the conspiracy, and the Union Pacific Railroad provided a special train for the event. Two partisan reporters were invited to accompany the expedition in order that the story would be presented with the correct bias.

'The mysterious train which left the city [Cheyenne] yesterday over the Union Pacific had a very important mission to fill,' reported *The Denver Sun* of 7 April, 1892, 'namely to get about 35 or 40 detectives to the northern part of Wyoming as rapidly as possible. The cattlemen . . . have formed an organization with the intention of exterminating the rustlers and have called on a detective agency for assistance. The UP officials here when asked about the train denied any knowledge of its having left the city.'

The invaders detrained at Casper, saddled their horses and rode toward Buffalo, the county seat of Johnson. But on the way they received information that Nate Champion and other rustlers were at the KC Ranch, only 12 miles distant. The raiders decided to deal with the much-wanted Champion before proceeding to Buffalo. They reached the KC soon after daybreak on 9 April and surrounded the place. Inside were Champion and his friend Nick Ray (who was also on the death list) and two trappers, the latter having taken shelter there for the night.

The trappers were the first to emerge; fortunately for them they were recognized as innocent visitors and were made prisoners by the raiders. When Nick Ray came out to take the morning air, he was shot down immediately and mortally wounded. Champion opened the door and, under a hail of bullets, managed to drag Ray inside. During the day-long siege that ensued, Champion, between returning the fire of his attackers, wrote a dramatic account of the event that was published in the Cheyenne *Daily Leader* on 14 April 1892:

'. . . It is now about two hours since the first shot. Nick is still alive; they are still shooting and are all around the house. Boys, there is bullets coming in like hail . . . They are shooting from the stable and river and back of the house. Nick is dead, he died about 9 o'clock. I see smoke down at the stable. I think they have fired it. I don't think they intend to let me get

A photograph of the invaders of the Johnson County Cattle War taken at Ft. D A Russell on 4 May 1892.

away this time. It is now about noon . . . I feel pretty lonesome just now. I wish there was someone here with me so we could watch all sides at once . . . It's about 3 o'clock now. There was a man in a buckboard and one on horseback just passed. They [the besiegers] fired on them as they went by. I don't know if they got any or not.'

The passing men managed to get away unhurt. One of them, Jack Flagg, happened to be high on the death list, although he did not know it at the time. He raced on to Buffalo and gave the alarm. The town quickly raised a defense

"THE INVA
JOHNSON COUNTY CATT
(FRANCIS E. WARR

No. 1 TOM SMITH	No 8 A.R. POWERS	No. 15 W.C. IRVINE
2 A.B. CLARKE	9 A.D. ADAMSON	16 BOB TISDALE
3 JN. LESLIE	10 C.A. CAMPBELL	17 JOE ELLIOTT
4 E.N. WHITCOMB	11 FRANK LABERTEAUX	18 JOHN TISDALE
5 D. BROOKE	12 PHIL DUFRAN	19 SCOTT DAVIS
6 W.B. WALLACE	13 MAJOR WOLCOTT	20 FRED DEBILLIER
7 CHAS FORD		

corps and, led by Red Angus, sheriff of Johnson County, rode out to combat the invaders. Johnson had asked for local military assistance, but to no avail. Meanwhile, time was running out for Nate Champion.

'It don't look as if there's much show of my getting away. I see 12 or 15 men. One looks like [name erased but believed to be Canton]. I don't know whether it is or not . . . They are shooting at the house now. If I had a pair of glasses I believe I would know some of those men. They are coming back, I've got to look out. Well, they have just got through shelling the house like hail. I heard them splitting wood. I guess they are going to fire the house tonight. I think I will make a break when night comes, if alive. Shooting again . . . The house is all fired. Goodbye, boys, if I never see you again. [Signed] Nathan D Champion.'

The valiant Texan, firing his Winchester, made a dash for freedom but 27 bullets cut him down. His killers read his account of the siege, probably deleted the mention of Canton, and gave it to one of the reporters. The Regulators rode on toward Buffalo but, on being warned that the outraged citizens of the town and dis-

TAKEN AT FT. D.A. RUSSELL
Y 4th 1892.
2. W.J. CLARKE
3. L.H. PARKER
4. TESCHMACHER
5. B.C. SCHULZE
6. W.H. TABOR
7. J.A. GARRETT

NO. 29 J. BARLINGS
. 30 M.A. MC NALLY
. 31 MIKE SHONSEY
. 32 DICK ALLEN
. 33 FRED HESSE
. 34 FRANK CANTON
. 35 WM LITTLE

NO. 36 JEFF MYNETT
. 37 BOB BARLINGS
. 38 S. SUTHERLAND
. 39 BUCK GARRETT
. 40 G.R. TUCKER
. 41 J.M. BENFORD
. 42 WILL ARMSTRONG

No. 5174

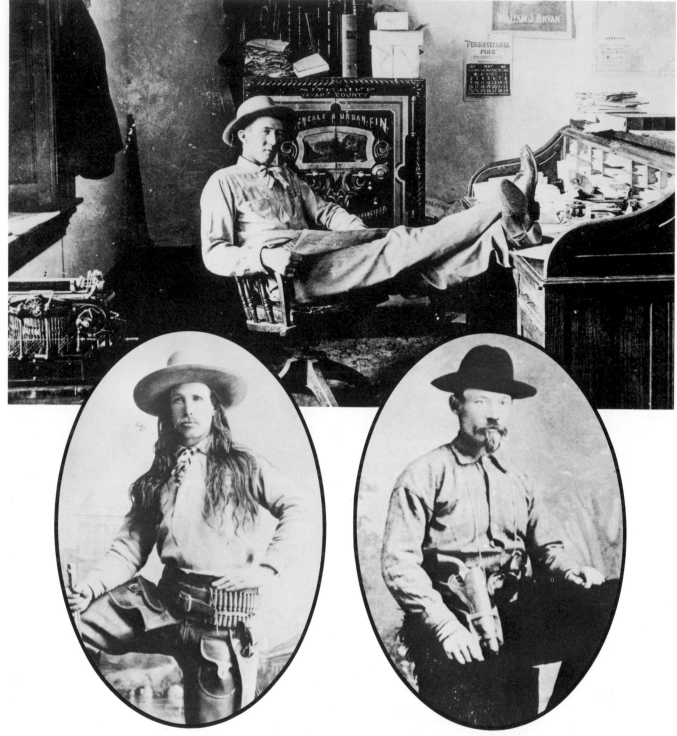

trict were heading for them, the invaders re-
treated to the nearby TA Ranch and barricaded
the place for a fight. Red Angus and his force of
grangers and nesters besieged the ranch for
three days. Meanwhile, news reached Cheyenne about the invaders' plight and their supporters began political wire-pulling to extricate
them from their sticky situation. Word was sent
to President Harrison in Washington, request-
ing military aid to suppress an insurrection in
Johnson County.

**Top: George Ruffner, the sheriff of Yavapai
County, Arizona, in 1897. Above left: Commodore
Perry Owens, the sheriff of Apache County,
Arizona. Above right: Ben Morrison, the cowboy
range detective, in a studio pose.**

In response to this unclarified appeal to
maintain law and order, three troops of the
Sixth Cavalry, commanded by Colonel Horn,
rode out of Fort McKinney and reached the TA
Ranch just in time to save the invaders. The

besiegers, weary of shooting at the fortified building, were on the point of dynamiting the place. Major Frank Wolcott came to meet Colonel Horn. 'I will surrender to you, sir,' said Wolcott, then indicating Sheriff Angus, 'but to that man, never!' Much to the anger of the besiegers, who would have exacted summary justice, the crestfallen invaders were taken as prisoners to Fort McKinney. And such was the power and political influence of the cattle kings that the case against the killer-raiders was never properly pursued and was eventually dismissed. However, the cattlemen had been taught a salutary lesson. The will of the little people of Johnson County had prevailed. Wyoming was no longer frontier land to be dominated by the armed force of a small group of powerful men to safeguard their own vested interests. The Johnson County War heralded the end of the 'Old West' ruled by the cattlemen and the 'New West' of the homesteader. By the turn of the century disputes and differences between the two factions were being settled in law courts or by mutual understanding and adaption to changing conditions.

One of the last of the old-time gunfighting range feuds was that between the Dewey cattle outfit and the Berry family of farmers in Rawlins County, northwest Kansas. In the 1890s C P Dewey from Chicago established the Oak Ranch in Rawlins, the largest cattle ranch in Kansas. In 1900 Chauncey Dewey, the 23-year-old son of C P, took personal charge of Oak Ranch and proceeded, ruthlessly, to expand the huge spread. Those homesteaders he could not buy out, he forced out by various means. Texas-born Chauncey was a cowboy in mind and manner and desired to be a cattle king of the old type. By 1903 Oak Ranch extended for 53 miles with a maximum width of 14 miles, and Chauncey wanted even more land. His wishes and demands were backed by a force of 50 armed cowboys. Dewey squeezed out nester after nester, usually by fencing them in until they had no way through without being harassed or arrested for trespassing. Most families gave up the struggle and moved on, allowing Dewey to move in. But not the Berry clan, who had lived on their different homesteads since 1885.

When Dewey cowboys started to fence and appropriate disputed land near their holdings, the armed Berrys appeared and ran them off. When Chauncey himself and his foreman rode out to investigate the matter, they were told to clear off in no uncertain manner. Chauncey brought legal action against the family and Roy Berry was fined for disturbing the peace. The feud intensified in hostile actions. Dewey cattle were shot, water holes and wells were poisoned, fences cut, and gunfire exchanged between the opposing parties. On 2 June 1903 an auction was held on the Alpheus Berry farm to settle a court judgment and Chauncey Dewey sent one of his cowboys to bid for a wooden water tank that he wanted. Two of the Berry boys stopped the man at the gate and threatened to shoot him if he stepped on Berry land. With the help of Sheriff McCulloch, the cowboy bid for the tank from neutral ground and bought the tank for five dollars, much to the Berry's chagrin.

The next day Chauncey Dewey and seven armed riders arrived at the Berry farm with a flat wagon to carry away the tank. But Roy, Burch, and Beach Berry were determined to stop them. Chauncey and some of his men took up positions behind a broken-down wall. The young cattle king leveled his rifle on the wall and called to the advancing brothers to 'stop right where you are.' Standing in the open, the Berrys pulled their six-shooters and started firing (that is, according to Dewey's account of the incident). Burch went down with a bullet in the brain. Roy Berry shot at Dewey and missed; Dewey fired back and struck Roy in the face. Alpheus Berry ran to the wall, attempted to grab Chauncey's rifle and got a bullet in the back of the head. Daniel Berry, the family patriarch, got caught in the gunfire and died. Beach Berry ran for the cover of the farmhouse and suffered a leg wound. Thirty minutes after the first shot the Dewey party rode away, leaving their sole fatality, a saddle horse, lying in the dirt with three dead men and one wounded.

Chauncey Dewey and two of his men were charged with murder and after a controversial trial were acquitted on the grounds of self-defense. Chauncey went on to become a prominent Republican politician and a friend of Theodore Roosevelt. In 1931 he opened the first dude ranch in Kansas.

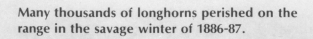
Many thousands of longhorns perished on the
range in the savage winter of 1886-87.

8
END OF THE OPEN RANGE

Here's luck to all ye homesteaders,
You've taken this country at last.
I hope you succeed in the future,
Like the cowboys did in the past.
The Wyoming Nester

By 1885 the open-range cattle business had reached its zenith. Millions of dollars had been invested in raising cattle on the Great Plains, much of the capital coming from England and Scotland, for there were huge profits to be made on beeves that fed on free grass. The cowboy had become a national figure. But the danger signs were there for those with eyes to see. The northern ranges were fully stocked, some of them overstocked, yet even more cattle were placed upon them and the once abundant grasslands could not support the ever increasing numbers of livestock, which now included millions of sheep. Cattlemen were producing more beef than the consumers required and beef prices began to fall. 'If you have any steers to shed, prepare to shed them now,' punned the Chicago *Daily Drover's Journal*.

'During the summer of 1885 more than 100,000 cattle were brought into Montana,' wrote Granville Stuart, pioneer rancher in that State, 'and by the fall the ranges were crowded. There was no way of preventing the overstocking of the ranges as they were free to all and men felt disposed to take big chances for the hope of large returns.'

The beef bonanza had been largely generated by books and journals describing the hefty profits to be had in raising cattle in the West. It was shown how a five-dollar calf could be matured at low cost on the rich grass of the public domain and sold at the end of four years for 40 or 50 dollars. An investment, then, of 5,000 dollars could in four years yield a net gain of 50,000 dollars. Eager investors poured money into the seemingly lucrative business; in 1883, in Wyoming alone, 20 companies were incorporated with a total capitalization of 12 million dollars. The big cattle companies, however, were riding for a fall, a disastrous fall from which most of them would never recover.

Theodore Roosevelt was one of many young gentlemen who invested money in the cow business. But he had more than just a financial interest in raising cattle. He loved the West and its people and gave his time and energy in personally supervising his ranching interests. He became a cowboy and shared the hard life of his hired hands and working partners. His period out West coincides with the peak and the ending of the open range cattle industry. Born in 1858 in New York City to a wealthy and influential family, he graduated from Harvard in 1880 and entered politics. Unlike his Dakota rancher-neighbor the Marquis de Mores, Roosevelt was neither tall nor handsome. He was, especially to cowboy eyes, physically unimpressive: short in stature, with bad eyesight that required thick spectacles; he was pale and skinny and spoke in a high-pitched voice. But he had plenty of guts, tremendous energy and a willingness to learn. In September, 1883 he visited Dakota for the first time, to hunt buffalo and other big game and while there he bought

An advertisement for Glidden's barbed wire, 1881.

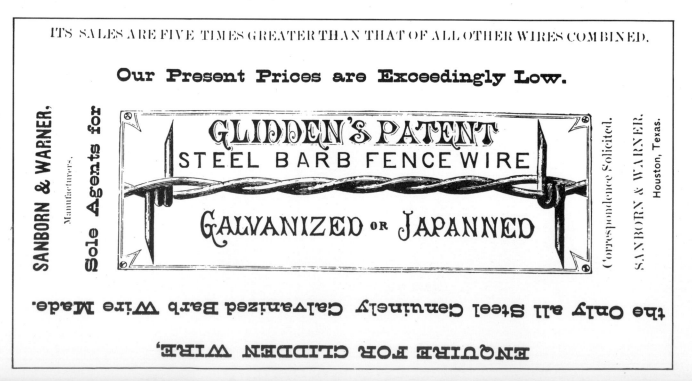

the Maltese Cross Ranch, some seven miles from the town of Medora, and stocked it with 400 cattle. On his return to New York he was elected to the State Assembly in November, 1883. Several months later he was struck by a double tragedy when both his wife and mother died. In search of solace he decided to occupy himself by investing further in the cattle business and returned to his ranch in Dakota.

'It was still the Wild West in those days,' Roosevelt wrote in his autobiography, 'the Far West of Owen Wister's stories and Frederic Remington's drawings, the West of the Indian and the buffalo-hunter, the soldier and the cow-puncher . . . It was a land of scattered ranches, of herds of long-horned cattle, and of reckless riders who unmoved looked in the eyes of life or of death.' Roosevelt the rancher immersed himself in his new life. 'For every day I have been here I have had my hands full,' he wrote his sister, Anna, 'the cattle have done well and I regard the outlook for making the business a success as being very hopeful. This winter I lost about 25 head from wolves, cold, etc., the others are in admirable shape, and I

Below: A cattle roundup in New Mexico in the 1920s. Right: Theodore Roosevelt poses in a photographer's studio.

have about 155 calves. I shall put on 1,000 more cattle and shall make it my regular business.'

In the summer of 1884 Roosevelt established another ranch, the Elkhorn, on the Little Missouri River some 35 miles north of Medora, and put two trusted foremen in charge. By 1886 his cattle numbered about 5,000 head. He was co-captain in the spring roundup of that year. 'I have been on the roundup for a fortnight,' he wrote his family, 'and really enjoy the work greatly . . . We breakfast at three every morning, and work from 16 to 18 hours a day, counting night guard; so I get pretty sleepy; but I feel strong as a bear.'

Although he was liable to issue orders strange to cowboy ears—such as 'Hasten forward quickly there!'—the bespectacled dude became a capable cattle boss and won the respect and loyalty of his cowhands and his neighbors. He often dined with the Marquis de Mores, whose aristocratic manners made the New York cow-

Top: The Texas longhorns were saved from extinction. These are found on the Wichita Mountains Wildlife Refuge near Cache, Oklahoma. Above: Herefords on the 1000-acre Curtice Martin Ranch in the Montana Rockies.

boy feel like a country bumpkin. On one occasion Roosevelt captured at gunpoint three men who had stolen his boat. In 1884 he was elected chairman of the Little Missouri Stockmen's Association, and in 1886 became its president.

But the halcyon years of the cattle kingdom were coming to an end. More and more homesteaders were moving into the open ranges, wanting their rightful share of the big country. They came primarily to cultivate the land and settle with their families and were encouraged

in this by government policy. 'I am in favor,' said Abraham Lincoln in February 1861, 'of settling the wild lands [of the trans-Mississippi West] into small parcels so that every poor man may have a home.' And on 20 May 1862 President Lincoln signed the Homestead Act which allowed any adult citizen or alien immigrant who was head of a family, on payment of a ten-dollar registration fee, to claim 160 acres (a quarter section) of surveyed and unappropriated public land and after residing upon and cultivating the land for five continuous years, to receive full title to the land on payment of a small further fee. Such homesteads were to be exempt from attachment for debt.

With growing apprehension the cattlemen

watched the incursion of the nester, or homesteader, into the public grasslands. With each passing year the cowmen saw the farms, enclosed by barbed wire fences, creep farther and farther westward into the cattle ranges. Violence flared between the nesters and the cattlemen. Again and again the little fellow was driven off, his fences cut and his crops and buildings destroyed. But the homesteader, with the law and numbers on his side, always returned to take up the struggle. The open range that stretched from Texas to Dakota was destined to become the farmer's domain.

The coming of the homesteader forced the could do little to curb this abuse of public land, except advise the homesteaders to cut the illegal fences, an action that resulted in conflict and bloodshed.

Three technical inventions were instrumental in changing the nature and the use of the open range: the chilled steel plow, the windmill, and barbed wire. The chilled steel plow, first produced in 1868 by James Oliver at South Bend, Indiana, provided the pioneer farmer with the first implement capable of cutting the tough prairie sod of the Western Plains. Surface water was precious and coveted on the Great Plains and he who possessed riparian

Top: A masked group cuts down a barbed wire fence in Nebraska in the 1880s. Bottom: The coming of barbed wire gave the cowboy a new job—riding the line, keeping it in order.

cattlemen to acquire proper title of land they had appropriated by occupation. A popular device was to induce cowboys to homestead a quarter section, usually on a river bank, then sell and sign it over to the cattle boss, and by homesteading a tract that controlled access to water they secured the best ranges. When the nesters began fencing their plots, the big ranchers also fenced off their range, and this led to vast areas of the public domain being illegally enclosed by the cattle companies. Because of loopholes in the laws and the political influence of the cattle kings, the government

rights was fortunate indeed. Where surface water was scarce, wells were sunk to tap the natural underground springs and reservoirs, and windmills, powered by the constantly blowing winds of the plains, were erected to pump the water to the surface. It is claimed that cattlemen were the first to employ the windmill pump; it certainly made possible the farmer's invasion and settlement of the cattle kingdom.

Wire fencing was the technical solution in terrain where the natural fence materials of wood and stone were scarce. In 1874 Joseph F Glidden, an Illinois farmer, patented his particular type of homemade barbed wire that proved the most practical and effective of the many types that had been devised; his improvement over the previous types was in the special barbed spur twisted through the double-strand wire. The initial use of barbed, or 'bob' wire as it was also called, by farmers and small ranchers to protect their privately-owned land, angered the free-ranging cattlemen, who called it 'devil's rope.' Nevertheless, cowmen adopted barbed wire fencing, which made it possible to keep cattle separate for selective breeding and the stringy Longhorn gave way to fine beef cattle such as Herefords and Durhams. Barbed wire provided the cowboy with a new duty—fence riding. They now spent much time patrolling the many miles of line to keep it in good order and repair.

Under the combined assault of the chilled steel plow, the water pumping windmill and barbed wire the open range cattle industry was inevitably doomed. The end was hastened by a hammer blow from the heavens: the terrible winter of 1886-87. Little rain fell during the summer of 1886 and grazing was poor on the parched and overstocked northern plains, yet cattle continued to arrive from the south. The fate of many stockmen depended upon a mild winter. What they got was a wicked winter of successive, devastating blizzards, the first of which struck with terrible effect late in November. The Dakota *Bismarck Tribune* described it as 'in many respects the worst on record.'

On 9 January 1887 it 'snowed steadily for 16 hours,' wrote Granville Stuart of Montana. 'The thermometer dropped to 22 degrees below zero ... and on the night of January 15 stood at 46 degrees below zero, and there was 16 inches of snow on the level. It was as though the Arctic regions had pushed down and enveloped us ... The cattle drifted before the storm and fat young steers froze to death along their trails ... We kept plenty of men on the range to look after [the cattle] as best they could, keeping them back from the rivers, and out of air holes and open channels in the ice, helping them out of drifts and keeping them in what shelter the cut banks and ravines offered.'

E C Abbott (Teddy Blue) was one of Stuart's cowboys who braved the blizzards—hell without the heat, he called it—to try and help the freezing cattle that drifted 'like gray ghosts with icicles hanging from their muzzles, eyes and ears.' Dressed in as much clothing as their aching bodies could carry, the cowboys rode the fury of the white storm and many of them perished. No sooner had a blizzard spent itself than it was followed by another. The ground was covered by a thick crust of ice that prevented the cattle from getting at the grass locked below. Without food and shelter the helpless animals died by the thousands.

Reports of the dreadful winter on the northern plains brought Theodore Roosevelt back from Europe. From Dakota he wrote to a friend: 'We have had a perfect smashup all through the cattle country of the northwest. The losses are crippling. For the first time I have been utterly unable to enjoy a visit to my ranch.' It was not until the spring thaw that the cattlemen were able to appraise their losses, which were indeed crippling if not crushing to many. Some had lost from 75 to 80 per cent of their stock. Cowboys reported riding the range all day without encountering a single live animal. Those that survived the terrible winter were in such emaciated condition that they were completely worthless.

'I am bluer than indigo about the cattle,' Roosevelt wrote his sister, 'it is even worse than I feared; I wish I was sure I would lose no more than half the money (80,000 dollars) I invested out here. I am planning to get out of it.' His total loss amounted to 50,000 dollars; he gradually withdrew from ranching and returned to full time politics. In 1898, with America at war with Spain, Theodore Roosevelt sold his remaining cattle interest to a part-

The Hold Up, a painting by the artist Frederic Remington.

ner and raised a regiment of cowboy cavalry to fight in Cuba.

Nature's merciless lesson was a salutary one. The enormous winter losses of livestock ruined many big outfits. Even the gigantic Swan Land and Cattle Company gave up the business in May 1887, followed soon by the Niobrara Cattle Company of Nebraska, and others. Granville Stuart suffered heavily. 'A business that had been fascinating to me before suddenly be-

came distasteful,' he wrote. 'I never wanted to own again an animal that I could not feed and shelter.' And he also withdrew from ranching. 'The experience from the financial standpoint,' opined the Bismarck *Weekly Tribune* of 26 February 1887, 'should teach stockmen to keep smaller herds and care for them well.'

The winter disaster of 1886-87 sounded the death knell to the range cattle business on anything like the large scale it had operated before. During the next ten years the cattle in Wyoming alone declined from nine million head to three million. 'There is not one cow-man,' wrote Julian Ralph on the Wyoming cattle business in June 1893, 'who does not know that small bunches of cattle, held in connection with agriculture, must take the place of the range cattle, because better grades of cattle can be bred, better meat produced, all risks will nearly disappear, and the expenses of the care of the cattle will not be a tithe of those of the old plan.'

Most of the big herds were gradually driven out and sold off, and the places of many of the early range operators were taken by ranchers with smaller herds, of about 200 head, who farmed as well as raised beef. With smaller outfits to manage, the ranchers began to economize on cowhands, food, wages, everything. 'The best of the old kind of cowboys,' wrote Julian Ralph, 'who had not become [cattle] owners or foremen, saloon-keepers or gamblers, or had not been shot, drifted away. Some of the smartest among them became "rustlers"—those cattle thieves whose depredations resulted in the [Johnson County] war in Wyoming last year. They insisted that they had to do it to live. From the cowboy standpoint it was time for the

business to languish . . . wages were low down; men had to cart hay and dump it around for winter food; settlers fenced in the streams . . . the range business was an obstruction to civilization, a bar to the development of the State, a thing only to be tolerated in a new and wild country.'

Times were a-changing. The trails of the long drives were plowed under and by the turn of the century the open-range cattle period was a thing of the past. Shorthorn and Hereford stock were introduced into the Southwest to improve the beef qualities, and Brahma cattle to produce animals more resistant to the Texas fever tick. By 1900 intensive cross-breeding had nearly erased the true Longhorn; it was saved from extinction by government and private endeavor and small herds were settled on wildlife preserves. In 1964 a group of Texas Longhorn owners organized the Texas Longhorn Breeders Association of America, and this historic breed is now established with more than 3,000 animals registered.

Cowboys return from a successful hunting trip. Their bag includes rabbits and a deer, (*Thanksgiving Dinner for the Ranch* by Remington).

The cowboys and the Longhorns
Who partnered in Eighty-four
Have gone to their last roundup
Over on the other shore
Songs of the Cowboys, N Howard Thorp

The heyday of the cowboy and the great cattle boom spanned twenty years, from 1870 to 1890. The transient rough-riders of the range and their wild cattle had been supplanted by the farmer-rancher and fine quality domestic beeves. 'It was right and necessary that this [open range cattle] life should pass,' wrote Theodore Roosevelt in his autobiography, 1913, 'for the safety of our country lies in its being made the country of the small home-maker. The great unfenced ranches, in the days of "free grass" . . . represented a temporary stage in our history . . . But the homesteaders, the permanent settlers, the men who took up each his own farm on which he lived and brought up his family, these represented from the National standpoint the

most desirable of all possible users of, and dwellers on, the soil. Their advent meant the breaking up of the big ranches; and the change was a National gain, although to some of us an individual loss.'

The trail-driving, range-riding cowboy faded into legend and his modern ranch hand counterpart is a different character. Buffalo Bill Cody and Theodore 'Teddy' Roosevelt both did much to popularize the cowboy as a romantic figure, the best of the American breed, an inimical figure of international interest and attraction. William Frederick Cody (1846-1917) was not a cowboy, but he had been a Pony Express rider, buffalo-hunter, Indian fighter and army scout. His Wild West Show, full of genuine cowboys and Indians, toured North America and Europe for 25 years performing before packed crowds and royalty.

First organized in 1883, Cody's colorful show featured original Western stars such as 'Bronco Bill' Irving; Buck Taylor, 'King of the Cowboys'; Johnny Baker, 'The Cowboy Kid'; crackshot Annie Oakley and the famous Sioux chief, Sitting Bull. A typical show would include rough riding and roping by cowboys; the Deadwood

Buffalo Bill's Wild West riders parade at the start of one of their performances at Omaha, Nebraska in 1907.

Roosevelt's Rough Riders distinguished themselves in the Spanish-American War in the action to take the San Juan Heights. Inset: A statue of 'Bucky' O'Neill.

Stage attacked by Indians and rescued in the nick of time by Buffalo Bill himself on a white horse; a re-enactment of 'Custer's Last Stand'; a sharp-shooting display by Annie Oakley; a horse race between cowboys and Indians, and many other events. It became the most popular and thrilling extravaganza of the period. Cody gave his last performance in November 1916. His Wild West show had many imitators. Hollywood cashed in on the cowboy and made him a cult, the Western movie becoming an essential ingredient of the international cinematic diet.

The formation of Roosevelt's Rough Riders is an interesting episode in the story of the cowboy. When the United States went to war with Spain in April 1898 and Congress authorized the recruitment of three volunteer cavalry regiments in the West and Southwest, Theodore Roosevelt immediately offered to raise one of them: 'In all the world there could be no better material for soldiers than that offered by these grim hunters of the mountains, these wild rough riders of the plains. They were accustomed to handling wild and savage horses; they were accustomed to following the chase with the rifle, both for sport and as a means of livelihood . . . almost all had, at one time or another, herded cattle and hunted big game. They were hardened to life in the open, and to shifting for themselves under adverse circumstances.'

Roosevelt's regiment of cowboy cavalry was recruited principally from Arizona, New Mexico, Texas, and the Indian Territory (Oklahoma). Its ranks also included a small number of wealthy sportsmen and collegiates from the eastern states, some of them friends of Roosevelt, prompting one reporter to describe the unit as 'the society page, financial column, and Wild West Show all wrapped up in one.' Officially designated the First US Volunteer Cavalry, the newspapers dubbed the regiment the 'Rough Riders' and the term came into official use. Roosevelt resigned his post as Assistant Secretary of the Navy in order to serve as the regiment's Lieutenant Colonel.

Left: *The Bronco Buster* by Frederic Remington, a statue given to Roosevelt by his regiment. Below: Roosevelt in his uniform as a Lieutenant Colonel in the cavalry.

Westerners flocked to join the Rough Riders and counted themselves lucky to be included in the selected number of 47 officers and 994 other ranks. Roosevelt mentions many of these characters in his book, *The Rough Riders.* 'There was little McGinty, the bronco-buster from Oklahoma, who had never walked a hundred yards if by any possibility he could ride . . . Smith, the bear hunter from Wyoming . . . Darnell and Wood of New Mexico, who could literally ride any horses alive.' The regiment also attracted a number of Texas Rangers and other peace officers. 'One of them,' wrote Roosevelt, 'Benjamin Franklin Daniels, had been Marshal of Dodge City.' Chris Madsen, a celebrated lawman of Oklahoma, served as Regimental Quartermaster Sergeant, and William 'Bucky' O'Neill, former sheriff of Yavapai County, Arizona, was appointed captain of A Troop.

The regiment assembled at San Antonio, Texas, prior to leaving for embarkation at Tampa, Florida, on 30 May 1898. 'The Rough Riders presented a very warlike appearance as

The cover of the sheet music of a popular song of 1898—*The Brave Rough Riders.* The tune was stolen from Carl Maria von Weber and the lyrics were by J W Lieb.

RESPECTFULLY DEDICATED TO
COL. THEODORE ROOSEVELT
AND

THE BRAVE
ROUGH RIDERS

BALLAD

MUSIC ARRANGED FROM C.M.v.WEBER
AND WORDS WRITTEN BY
J.W. LIEB.

they strolled about the depot before leaving,' reported the *San Antonio Express.* 'Their belts were loaded with ammunition, and their carbines and six-shooters were slung to their belts, ready for action.' The regiment soon collected another nickname, 'Teddy's Terrors.' Roosevelt himself was pleased with his men's appearance. 'Their uniform suited them,' he wrote. 'In their slouch hats, blue flannel shirts, brown trousers, leggings, and boots, with handkerchiefs knotted loosely around their necks, they looked exactly as a body of cowboy cavalry should look.'

At Tampa all was confusion. There was no plan to embark the men and no staff on hand to direct the movement. It took four days to embark the army of some 17,000—an operation which if properly organized could have been done easily in eight hours. This was typical of the lack of planning that plagued the US Army throughout the war. There was a shortage of transport ships and consequently the Rough Riders had to leave four troops behind and all the horses of the other ranks, only the officers' mounts being taken. When the regiment landed in Cuba they fought dismounted, which must have upset most of the cowboys, especially Bill McGinty.

On 1 July 1898 Teddy's Terrors took part in the famous action to take the San Juan Heights, a fortified ridge in front of Santiago. General Shafter, the army commander, ordered a frontal attack. This was Roosevelt's 'crowded hour.' On horseback, fully exposed to heavy fire, he led his pedestrian Rough Riders, and various units of other regiments up Kettle Hill, a height separate from the main ridge. The troopers stormed the hill and captured it. Roosevelt won military glory and his cowboy soldiers had distinguished themselves. The 'Splendid Little War' was well covered by reporters in the field, including Frederic Remington, the celebrated artist of the Old West. Almost overnight Roosevelt became a national hero and his Rough Riders shared the fame.

In August 1898 Spain agreed to get out of Cuba and the war was virtually over. The Rough Riders were shipped home and the regiment disbanded on 15 September at Montauk Point, New York. The men had developed much admiration and love for Roosevelt and on

Homesteaders in front of their sod house. The sod bricks were often the only building material available on the prairie. Left: A typical wind pump of the West. The use of these pumps to raise water for livestock and irrigation of crops greatly improved the agricultural productivity of the small farmer. Right: A cowboy on a poster advertising Sunset magazine in 1904.

the day before disbandment they presented him with a fine equestrian bronze, 'The Bronco-buster,' by Remington. In his book *The Rough Riders*, Roosevelt tells of an amusing cowboy incident at Montauk Point.

'Some troopers of the [regular] Third Cavalry were getting ready for mounted drill when one of their horses escaped, having thrown the rider. This attracted the attention of some of our men and they strolled over to see the trooper remount. He was instantly thrown again, the horse, a huge, vicious sorrel, being one of the worst buckers I ever saw; and none of his comrades were willing to ride the animal.'

Roosevelt's cowboys jeered and mocked the regular troopers, and in response were dared to ride the rogue horse themselves. The challenge

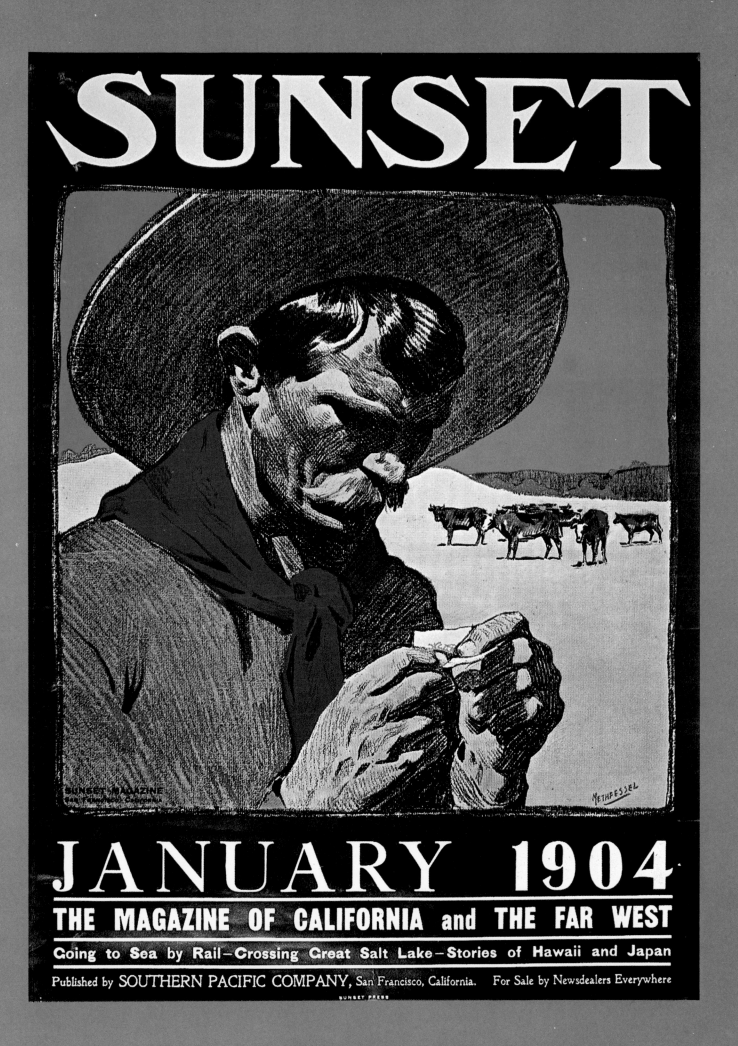

was instantly accepted, the only question being as to which of the dozen noted bronco-busters should have the honor of mounting the bucker. The choice was Tom Darnell of New Mexico. And it was agreed that the ride should take place the next day when the horse would be fresh—and mean.

'The majority of both regiments turned out on a big open flat in front of my tent—brigade headquarters,' wrote Roosevelt. 'The result was that after as fine a bit of rough-riding as one would care to see . . . Darnell came off victorious, his seat never having been shaken. After this almost every day we had exhibitions of bronco-busting in which all the crack riders of the regiment vied with one another, riding not only all our bad horses but any other horse which was deemed bad in any of the other regiments.'

Below: Bruce Ford, the World Bareback Bronc Champion, 1980.

Riding high on his war record, Roosevelt went on to become Governor of New York, was elected Vice-President of the United States in 1900, succeeded the assassinated McKinley the following year, and remained in office till 1909. He never forgot his beloved Rough Riders and helped them where he could and sent money to the needy. Bill McGinty and some others joined Buffalo Bill's Wild West show and, billed as 'Roosevelt's Rough Riders,' did a regular rendition of the 'Battle of San Juan Hill,' with Buffalo Bill playing the role of his friend Teddy Roosevelt. Chris Madsen was appointed a deputy US Marshal, and Tom Darnell, the bucking hero, was shot dead in a gunfight.

The modern cowboy, or ranch hand, still rides a horse and handles cattle, but a jeep or pickup truck is as important to him as a four-legged mount. He still ropes and brands calves

Below center: The Buffalo Bill show re-enacts a battle, 1907.

and cuts out cattle from the herd, but the well-bred, docile creatures of today in no way compare with the rough, mean-tempered Longhorns of long ago. The modern ranch hand is more a jack-of-all-trades than pure cowboy. His jobs are many and varied. They include fixing fences, making and feeding hay to the cattle in winter, breaking ice on the water holes, bringing cows to the barn to calve, helping with artificial insemination, branding and innoculating cattle held in a mechanical 'squeeze' contraption, oiling the windmills and repairing the pumps and engines.

There's never a cowboy who couldn't be
  throwed,
Never a bronc that couldn't be rode.
  Traditional rodeo saying

Below: Paul Tierney, the All Around Cowboy Champion of 1980. Right: Sid Wilson, 101-year-old cowboy, and former bronc rider with Buffalo Bill.

Rodeo keeps alive and kicking the spirit of the hard-riding cowboy of the Old West. Today it is a multi-million-dollar sport attended by more than ten million spectators annually throughout the nation. The word 'rodeo' comes from the Spanish *rodear*, to encircle or round up. It is claimed that the first organized rodeo took place in Pecos, Texas, in 1884 when cowboys held roughriding and cattle-roping competitions to celebrate the Fourth of July. The idea caught on and spread throughout the cattle country. Rodeo entered the big league of American sport in 1936 when the present Rodeo Cowboys Association was formed, which brought uniform regulations and professional status to the sport.

Right: A demonstration of bull riding at the Cheyenne Frontier Days Rodeo in Cheyenne, Wyoming. In this event, only one hand may be used. The man in the striped shirt is a clown.
Below: A demonstration of bareback bronco riding at a 1976 rodeo held in Deadwood, South Dakota. The rules for this event state that only one hand can be used.

There are five standard events in a rodeo show: saddle bronc riding, bareback riding, bull riding, calf roping, and steer wrestling, the latter is also known as bulldogging, an exercise in strength and courage originated by Bill Pickett at the turn of the century. Top riders travel all over North America to compete in some 100 rodeos every year. The big money prizes make the sport highly competitive. The rider who wins the most prize money in the season, which ends with the National Finals Rodeo in December, is named World Champion All-Around Cowboy.

Left: More bull riding. This time the rodeo is in Greeley, Colorado. Once the rider has been thrown, it is the responsibility of the clowns to distract the bull. Below: One of the most outstanding of all bull riders is Randy Majers. Here he is seen riding the bull nicknamed 'Al Capone,' probably on account of his fierce temper.

INDEX

ACKNOWLEDGMENTS

The author and publisher would like to thank the following people who have helped in the preparation of this book: Thomas G Aylesworth, who edited it; Elfriede Hueber, who drew the map; Karin Knight, who prepared the index.

PICTURE CREDITS

All pictures were supplied by Peter Newark's **Western Americana**. The author would like to thank the following:

American Quarter Horse Assn: 82-83.
Amoco Oil Co: 13 (main), 124-25.
Anton Jann Collection: 152 (top left).
Arizona Historical Society: 136 (top and lower left).
Barney Hubbs Collection: 105 (top right), 115.
Burlington Northern, Inc: 100 (right), 142 (below).
California Historical Society: 26-27.
Colt Industries Firearms Div: 18, 19 (top inset), 106 (second from top), 112 (bottom).
David Allen: 156, 157.
David Lee Guss: 155 (right).
Denver Public Library Western History Dept: 77 (left), 146 (top).
The Dobie Collection, University of Texas, Austin: 33 (center top).
Harold's Club Gun Collection, Reno, Nev: 105 (bottom), 106 (top and bottom).
James Fain photograph supplied by the R J Reynolds Tobacco Co: 81, 154 (left).
Jane Carter's Camera Center, Prescott, Ariz: 148 (inset).
Justin Boot Co: 75 (below), 94 (top left).
Kansas State Historical Society: 41, 44-45, 48, 49, 60, 77 (right), 78-79, 85 (second from left), 102-103, 110, 111 (top).
Library of Congress: 35.
Kennedy Galleries, Inc, New York City: 31 (inset), 55 (below).
Montana Historical Society: 52-53, 74, 85 (third from left).

The National Archives: 67, 122, 123 (top right), 153 (top and bottom).
National Park Service, US Dept. of the Interior: 18 (top), 19 (inset below), 141 (above).
Nebraska State Historical Society: 101.
Olin Corp, Winchester-Western Div: 107 (bottom), 117.
Oliver Yates Collection: 13, 22, 33 (top right), 42 (right), 76, 96 (bottom), 118.
Professional Rodeo Cowboys Association, Inc: 155.
Remington Arms Co, Inc: 107 (second from bottom).
Solomon D Butcher Collection, Nebraska State Historical Society: 69 (below).
Sotheby Park Bernet: 107 (top).
Stetson Hat Co, Inc: 94 (top right).
Title Insurance and Trust Co, Los Angeles: 19 (below).
Union Pacific Railroad Museum: 88 (top and center).
United Artists Corp: 113, 132.
University of Texas, El Paso: 11 (center).
University of Wyoming: 133 (bottom), 134-35.
Valley National Bank of Arizona: 145.
Warner Brothers, Inc: 116.
Western History Collections, University of Oklahoma Library: 20 (left), 64.
Whitney Gallery of Western Art: 95 (inset).
Wichita Mountains Wildlife Refuge: 142 (top).
Woolaroc Museum, Bartlesville, Okla: 1, 16 (top), 19 (top).
Wyoming State Archives and Historical Department: 2-3, 69 (top), 88 (bottom), 108, 114, 147, 154-55.

The Pierce-Arrow